Quick Start Guides

The Essential
SLOW COOKER
Recipe Book

100 Delicious & Nutritious Slow Cooker Recipes

**Easy Calorie-Counted Cookbook
To Make Your Life Simpler**

First published in 2020 by Erin Rose Publishing

Text and illustration copyright © 2020 Erin Rose Publishing

Design: Julie Anson

All Rights Reserved. No part of this publication may be reproduced, stored in a retrieval system or transmitted by any form or by any means, electronic, recording or otherwise without the prior permission in writing from the publishers. Unauthorised reproduction of any part of this publication by any means including photocopying is an infringement of copyright.

DISCLAIMER: This book is for informational purposes only and not intended as a substitute for the medical advice, diagnosis or treatment of a physician or qualified healthcare provider. The reader should consult a physician before undertaking a new health care regime and in all matters relating to his/her health, and particularly with respect to any symptoms that may require diagnosis or medical attention.

While every care has been taken in compiling the recipes for this book we cannot accept responsibility for any problems which arise as a result of preparing one of the recipes. The author and publisher disclaim responsibility for any adverse effects that may arise from the use or application of the recipes in this book. Some of the recipes in this book include nuts and eggs. If you have an egg or nut allergy it's important to avoid these. It is recommended that children, pregnant women, the elderly or anyone who has an immune system disorder avoid eating raw eggs.

CONTENTS

Introduction 1
Making The Most Of Your Slow Cooker 2
Breakfast & Light Meal Recipes 5
Spiced Apple Porridge 6
French Toast Breakfast Casserole 7
Meaty Breakfast Casserole 8
Vegetarian Breakfast Casserole 9
Quinoa & Coconut Porridge 10
Coconut, Almond & Raspberry Porridge 11
Feta & Tomato Frittata 12
Soup Recipes 13
Turkey & Vegetable Broth 14
Tomato & Red Pepper Soup 15
Lentil & Vegetable Soup 16
French Onion Soup & Cheese Croutons 17
Spicy Chicken & Chickpea Soup 18
Seafood Chowder 19
Minestrone Soup 20
Cream of Pumpkin Soup 21
Tomato & Quinoa Soup 22
Thai Curry Soup 23
Cheesy Vegetable Soup 24
Pea Soup 25
Creamy Celeriac Soup 26

Main Meals 27
Chicken, Chorizo & Vegetable Casserole 28
Slow Cooked Spiced Ham 29
Beef Pot Roast 30
Chicken & Butternut Squash 31
Thai Salmon Curry 32
Citrus Spiced Pork Fillet 33
Chicken & Mushroom Casserole 34
Sweet & Sour Chicken 35
Prawn & Lemon Risotto 36
Chestnut Mushroom & Red Pepper Risotto 37
Lemon Chicken 38
Chinese Beef & Broccoli 39
Creamy Quinoa & Tomato Chicken 40
Jambalaya 41
Lamb Shanks 42
Tender 'Roast' Chicken 43
Pork, Apple & Ginger Chops 44
Tandoori Chicken 45
Paella 46
Chicken 'Fried' Rice 47
Chinese Pulled Pork 48
Pork Vindaloo 49
Bolognese 50
Aromatic Pork Ribs 51
Chicken Tagine 52
Beef & Barley Stew 53
Chilli Chicken & Quinoa 54
Chicken Fajitas 55

Lamb Hotpot	56
Coconut & Coriander Chicken	57
Goulash	58
Cajun Pulled Pork	59
Beef & Root Vegetables	60
Chinese Chicken & Noodles	61
Lamb Moussaka	62
Tender Five-Spice Beef	63
Beef Bourguignon	64
Lamb & Mango Tikka	65
Chicken Cacciatore	66
Pulled Chicken & Lettuce Wraps	67
Pork, Mustard & Apple Casserole	68
Chicken Tikka Masala	69
Pork Curry	70
Chicken & Ham Pie	71
Slow Cooked Meat Loaf	72
Salmon & Cannellini Mash	73
Chicken Stroganoff	74
Chicken Wings	75
Sausage Cassoulet	76
Spanish Chorizo & Peppers	77
Smoked Haddock & Pea Purée	78
Turkey Meatballs & Tomato Sauce	79
Satay Chicken	80
Sausage Casserole	81
Vegetarian Dishes	**83**
Slow Cooked Mac & Cheese	84
Vegetarian Lasagne	85

Slow Cooked Dahl 86
Sweet Potato, Peppers & Chickpeas 87
Garlic, Tomato & Mushroom Spaghetti 88
Cauliflower Korma 89
Caribbean Citrus Squash 90
Slow Cooked 'Baked' Potatoes 91
Stuffed Peppers 92
Butternut Squash & Bean Casserole 93
Vegetable & Cannellini Bean Rice 94
Ratatouille 95
Baked Beans 96
Braised Savoy Cabbage & Peas 97
Slow Cooked Autumn Vegetables 98
Red Cabbage 99
Sugar-Free Pasta Sauce 100
Cranberry & Orange Sauce 101

Dessert & Pudding Recipes 103
Chocolate Brownies 104
Lemon & Coconut Rice Pudding 105
Chocolate Rice Pudding 106
Banana Bread 107
Stuffed Apples 108
Poached Peaches 109
Fruit Compote 110
Fresh Custard & Raspberries 111

Introduction

Slow cooking has never been so easy! This comprehensive cookbook provides you with 100 tasty and easy recipes which anyone can cook. Choose from simple breakfasts, curries, soups, stews, casseroles, and even desserts, the whole family will love!

Spend less time in the kitchen and enjoy more free time. Just add a few ingredients to your slow cooker and you can let it take care of the rest. It takes very little preparation and it's a great way of healthy eating. Using a slow cooker is a life hack which lets you get on with life and still enjoy delicious meals when you're ready for them.

If you want to lose weight and eat healthily, you can avoid junk food, additives, excess salt and empty calories and cook your own favourite meals using a slow cooker. That way you know exactly what fresh, nutritious ingredients have gone into your meals and your slow cooker will tenderise and blend the flavours. Home cooking is more enjoyable when it's made simple.

Do you get the most out of your slow cooker? Sometimes we just need a few ideas and a little inspiration to spice up meal times. Many slow cooked meals only require a few minutes preparation and you can save time and effort cooking. Experiment and expand your range of recipes and enjoy rice and pasta dishes, pies and casseroles, frittatas and desserts with barely any effort.

Making The Most Of Your Slow Cooker

Slow cookers, which are also known as crockpots, come in a variety of sizes. The important thing is to follow the guidelines specific to your model of slow cooker. For instance, many of them don't require pre-heating but check your manufacturer's instructions in case yours does. If so, allow for this in the preparation time. Preparation time doesn't usually take long but cooking time does take longer and bear in mind that the cooking times in this slow cooker recipe book are approximate. Always check that food is completely cooked but as you're putting your slow cooker on for a few hours, this shouldn't be a problem. Allowing longer for cooking time shouldn't impact flavour and if anything it can add to it, providing your machine isn't left on too high or without liquid.

Slow cooking infuses the flavours and improves the taste and tenderness of food. If you are cooking for a family it's ideal and it makes batch cooking for larger groups easier too. It's a great way to use up left-overs, especially if you're cooking for one and you can freeze it in portions. Even leftover gravies and sauces can be frozen then defrosted to be used in other meals. You might find it handy to freeze meals into single portions which can be removed, thawed and completely reheated later.

Slow cookers usually have 3 or 4 settings ranging from warm to high. Bear in mind that if you wish to preheat your slow cooker, do so using the highest setting which will take less time, remembering you may wish to lower the setting during the slow-cooking process. You can choose your slow cooker setting according to your schedule but make sure you allow enough cooking time for fish, chicken and meat dishes to make sure it is cooked and also that it's succulent and tender. You can always test your food using a kitchen thermometer or skewer.

Always use some liquid in the slow cooker to prevent it sticking or burning. You can be innovative and use your slow cooker as a ban marie to make breads and desserts. Try not to keep removing the lid of your cooker as you may need to

The Essential Slow Cooker Recipe Book

increase the cooking time. Also, if you remove the lid frequently you may be losing a lot of moisture so you may need to add a little extra if it looks like it's drying. Many of our recipes do not require 'browning' in a pan before transferring it to the slow cooker but in some cases it can improve the appearance of the meat but it's up to you. If an excessive amount of liquid or fat comes from your dish you can scoop some of it off.

Keep a plentiful supply of fresh produce including plenty of vegetables, eggs, cheese and meats. You can do this in the fridge or the freezer and while our recipes mostly include the use of fresh vegetables you can swap these for the frozen variety if you like. Also you can use chicken, fish and meat from the freezer too if you don't want to overstock your fridge.

BREAKFAST & LIGHT MEAL RECIPES

Spiced Apple Porridge

Ingredients

- 100g (3½ oz) oats
- 25g (1oz) butter
- 2 apples, peeled, cored and chopped
- 2 teaspoons ground cinnamon
- ½ teaspoon ground nutmeg
- ½ teaspoon salt
- 600mls (1 pint) water
- 250mls (9 fl oz) milk
- Butter for greasing

SERVES 2

352 calories per serving

Method

Coat the inside of the slow cooker with the butter. Add all the ingredients to the slow cooker and stir well. Cook overnight on low for a delicious, warming porridge in the morning. You can also easily increase the quantities to make a larger batch and store it in the fridge, ready to use.

French Toast Breakfast Casserole

Ingredients

50g (2oz) butter

8 slices of wholemeal bread

6 eggs

2 large bananas, peeled and mashed

1 teaspoon vanilla extract

1/4 teaspoon cinnamon

1/4 teaspoon nutmeg

350mls (12fl oz) double cream (or crème fraîche)

Butter for greasing

SERVES 4

372 calories per serving

Method

Grease the inside bowl of a slow cooker with a little butter. Spread each of the slices of bread with butter then cut them into triangles. Lay the bread over the bottom of the slow cooker. In a bowl, combine the eggs, cream, vanilla, cinnamon and nutmeg. Pour the mixture over the bread and sprinkle with a little cinnamon and nutmeg. Cook on low for 4 hours or on high for 2 hours. As an alternative, try replacing the bananas with an apple or berries and have fun experimenting with your favourite.

Meaty Breakfast Casserole

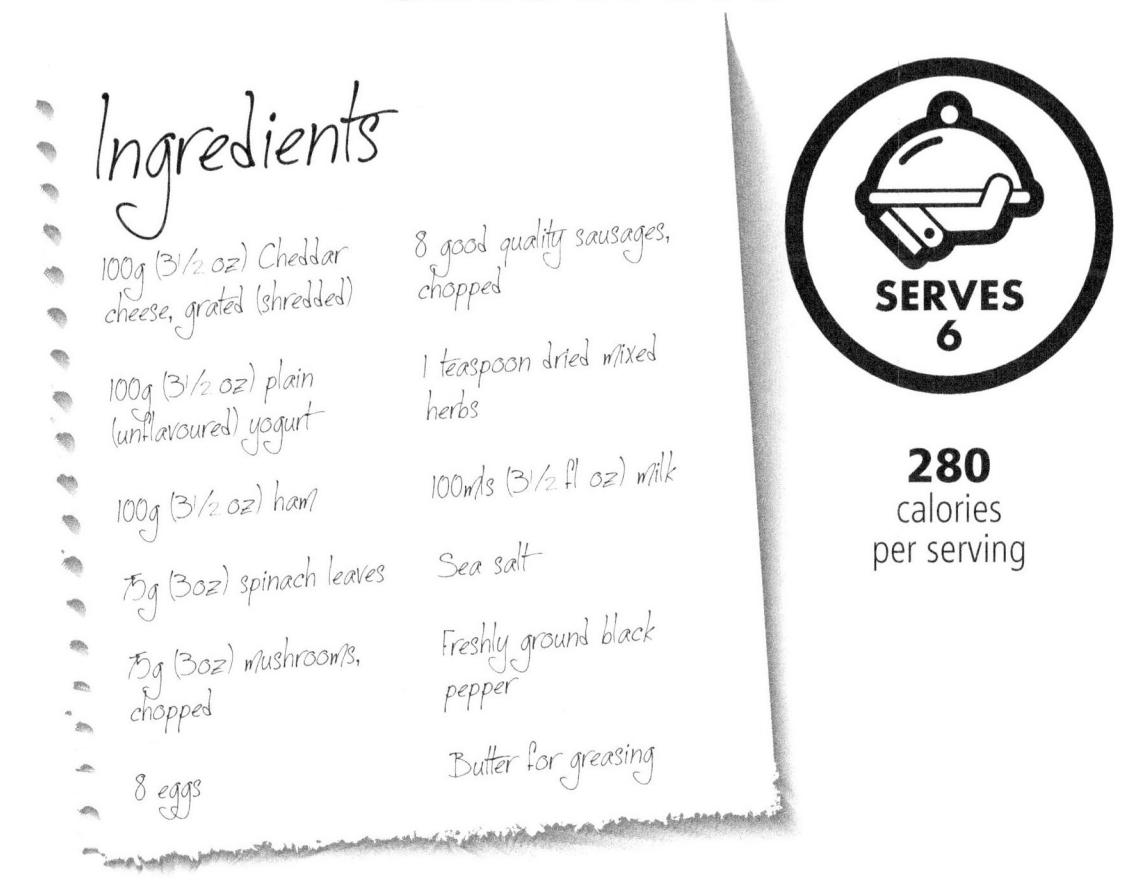

Ingredients

- 100g (3½ oz) Cheddar cheese, grated (shredded)
- 100g (3½ oz) plain (unflavoured) yogurt
- 100g (3½ oz) ham
- 75g (3oz) spinach leaves
- 75g (3oz) mushrooms, chopped
- 8 eggs
- 8 good quality sausages, chopped
- 1 teaspoon dried mixed herbs
- 100mls (3½ fl oz) milk
- Sea salt
- Freshly ground black pepper
- Butter for greasing

SERVES 6

280 calories per serving

Method

Grease and line the inside of the slow cooker bowl with grease-proof paper. In a large bowl, combine the eggs with the milk, yogurt and herbs. Add in the cheese, sausages, ham (or bacon), mushrooms and spinach. Season with salt and pepper. Pour the mixture into the slow cooker and cook on low for at least 4-5 hours or on high for 2-3 hours.

The Essential Slow Cooker Recipe Book

Vegetarian Breakfast Casserole

Ingredients

75g (1½ lb) potatoes, peeled and finely sliced

150g (5oz) Cheddar cheese, grated (shredded)

8 eggs

2 teaspoons mustard

1 clove of garlic, crushed

1 teaspoon pepper

1 teaspoon salt

1 teaspoon dried mixed herbs

1 teaspoon sweet paprika

1 onion, peeled and finely chopped

1 red pepper (bell pepper) deseeded and chopped

1 yellow pepper (bell pepper) deseeded and chopped

1 small head of broccoli, roughly chopped

600mls (1 pint) milk

Butter for greasing

SERVES 6

383 calories per serving

Method

Grease and line the inside bowl of a slow cooker with grease-proof paper. Line the potato slices over the bottom of the pot. Scatter a layer of peppers, onion, broccoli and cheese on top. Add another layer of sliced potatoes and scatter the remaining vegetables on top. In a bowl, mix together the eggs, mustard, garlic, salt, pepper, paprika, herbs and milk. Pour the egg mixture over the ingredients in the slow cooker. Cook on low for 4-5 hours.

Quinoa & Coconut Porridge

Ingredients

- 150g (5oz) quinoa
- 1 teaspoon vanilla extract
- 1 teaspoon stevia sweetener (optional)
- ½ teaspoon cinnamon
- 400mls (14fl oz) water
- 200mls (7fl oz) coconut milk
- Pinch of salt

SERVES 2

240 calories per serving

Method

Place all of the ingredients into the bowl of a slow cooker and stir well. Cook on a low setting for around 7-8 hours. This makes a high protein alternative to oaty porridge and you can add toppings such as berries or chopped nuts.

Coconut, Almond & Raspberry Porridge

Ingredients

250g (9oz) fresh raspberries

100g (3½ oz) oats

2 tablespoons desiccated (shredded) coconut

1 tablespoon ground almonds (almond meal/almond flour)

1 teaspoon vanilla extract

½ teaspoon cinnamon

Pinch of salt

600mls (1 pint) water

250mls (9 fl oz) milk

SERVES 2

374 calories per serving

Method

Place the oats, coconut, almonds, cinnamon, salt, vanilla, water and milk into the bowl and mix well. Cook on low overnight. When ready to serve, scatter the raspberries into the porridge and save a few as garnish. Eat straight away.

Feta & Tomato Frittata

Ingredients

- 150g (5oz) mushrooms, sliced
- 125g (4oz) feta cheese, crumbled
- 100g (3½ oz) cherry tomatoes (halved)
- 8 eggs
- 4 spring onions (scallions) chopped
- 2 tablespoons grated (shredded) Parmesan cheese
- 1 large handful of fresh spinach, finely chopped
- 1 tablespoon butter
- ½ teaspoon mixed herbs
- ¼ teaspoon salt
- ¼ teaspoon pepper
- Butter for greasing

SERVES 4

245 calories per serving

Method

Coat the bowl of a slow cooker with butter. Whisk the eggs in a large bowl then stir in all the remaining ingredients. Pour the egg mixture into the slow cooker. Cook on high for 2 hours or on low for around 4 hours. Serve and enjoy.

SOUP RECIPES

Turkey & Vegetable Broth

Ingredients

- 450g (1lb) fresh turkey breast steaks, chopped
- 400g (14oz) tin of chopped tomatoes
- 200g (7oz) brown lentils, rinsed
- 100g (3½ oz) pearl barley
- 75g (3oz) cabbage, finely chopped
- 3 stalks of celery, finely chopped
- 2 cloves of garlic, chopped
- 1 carrot, peeled and diced
- 1 onion, peeled and chopped
- 1 handful of fresh spinach leaves
- 1 teaspoon dried mixed herbs
- 2 tablespoons tomato purée (paste)
- 1 small handful of fresh parsley, chopped
- 1200mls (2 pints) chicken stock (broth)
- 300mls (½ pint) hot water
- Sea salt
- Freshly ground black pepper

SERVES 6

208 calories per serving

Method

Place all of the ingredients, except the parsley, salt and pepper, into a slow cooker and stir well. Cook on high for around 6 hours. If you prefer your soup thinner you can add a little extra hot water. Sprinkle in the parsley and stir well. Season with salt and pepper. Serve into bowls.

The Essential Slow Cooker Recipe Book

Tomato & Red Pepper Soup

Ingredients

350g (12oz) tomatoes on the vine, stalk removed and chopped

2 red peppers (bell peppers), deseeded and chopped

2 onions, peeled and chopped

1 sweet potato, peeled and chopped

2 cloves of garlic, crushed

400mls (14fl oz) hot vegetable stock (broth)

Sea salt

Freshly ground black pepper

SERVES 4

105 calories per serving

Method

Place all of the vegetables into a slow cooker and pour the hot vegetable stock (broth) on top. Cook on high for around 4 hours or cook on low for 6-7 hours. Season with salt and pepper. Using a hand blender, process the soup until until smooth. Serve and enjoy.

Lentil & Vegetable Soup

Ingredients

- 100g (3½ oz) red lentils
- 3 stalks of celery, chopped
- 3 cloves of garlic, crushed
- 1 carrot, peeled and roughly chopped
- 1 onion, peeled and roughly chopped
- 1 sweet potato, peeled and chopped
- 1 potato, peeled and chopped
- 1 leek, washed and chopped
- 1 bay leaf
- 900mls (1 ½ pints) hot vegetable stock (broth)
- 2 teaspoons tomato purée (paste)
- 2 teaspoons fresh parsley, chopped
- Sea salt
- Freshly ground black pepper

SERVES 4

106 calories per serving

Method

Place all of the lentils and vegetables and the garlic into a slow cooker and pour in the vegetable stock (broth). Stir in the tomato purée (paste) and bay leaf. Cook on high for around 6 hours or on low for 8-9 hours. Sprinkle in the parsley and season with salt and pepper. Remove the bay leaf and serve.

French Onion Soup & Cheese Croutons

Ingredients

- 100g (3½ oz) Gruyère cheese, grated (shredded)
- 6 large onions, peeled and finely sliced
- 4 slices baguette
- 3 cloves garlic, crushed
- 2 tablespoons olive oil
- 2 tablespoons Worcester sauce
- 750mls (1¼ pints) hot chicken stock (broth)
- Pinch salt
- Freshly ground black pepper

SERVES 4

295 calories per serving

Method

Place the oil, onions, garlic, Worcester sauce, stock (broth), salt and pepper into a slow cooker and stir the mixture really well. Cook on low for around 4 hours. When ready to serve, place the bread slices under a hot grill (broiler) and toast it on one side. Turn it over and sprinkle some cheese on top then return it to the grill until the cheese has melted. Serve the cheese crouton on top of the soup and eat straight away.

Spicy Chicken & Chickpea Soup

Ingredients

- 450g (1lb) chicken fillets, cut into chunks
- 400g (14oz) tinned chopped tomatoes
- 1 red pepper (bell pepper), de-seeded and chopped
- 1 onion, peeled and chopped
- 2 cloves of garlic, crushed
- 1 teaspoon paprika
- 1 teaspoon ground cumin
- 1 teaspoon Harissa paste
- 275g (10oz) tinned chickpeas, drained
- 750mls (1½ pints) chicken stock (broth)
- 2 tablespoons fresh coriander (cilantro) leaves, chopped

SERVES 4

308 calories per serving

Method

Place the chicken into a slow cooker and add in the vegetables. Pour in the stock (broth) and stir in the garlic, spices and Harissa paste. Cook the soup on low for 8 hours or on high for around 5 hours. Sprinkle in the fresh coriander and stir. Serve on its own or with a dollop of plain (unflavoured) yogurt.

Seafood Chowder

Ingredients

450g (1oz) cod fillets, roughly chopped

400g (14oz) tin of chopped tomatoes

275g (10oz) potatoes, peeled and diced

25g (1oz) butter, melted

3 tablespoons plain flour (all-purpose flour)

2 stalks of celery, finely chopped

2 teaspoons dried parsley

1 onion, peeled and chopped

1 carrot, peeled and finely diced

1 teaspoon salt

1 teaspoon white pepper

600mls (1 pint) fish or vegetable stock (broth)

50mls (2fl oz) double cream (heavy cream)

Splash of tabasco sauce

SERVES 4

338 calories per serving

Method

Place the fish, potatoes, onion, celery and carrot into a slow cooker. Sprinkle in the salt, pepper, parsley, tomatoes and a splash of tabasco sauce. Pour in the stock (broth) and stir all the ingredients well. Cook on low for 7 hours or on high for 3 hours. In a small bowl, mix together the butter, cream and flour until it becomes smooth then slowly add the mixture the chowder, stirring continuously. Cook for 40 minutes. Serve into bowls and enjoy.

Minestrone Soup

SERVES 4

145 calories per serving

Ingredients

- 400g (14oz) tinned chopped tomatoes
- 275g (10oz) tinned kidney beans, drained
- 50g (2oz) spaghetti, broken up
- 50g (2oz) green beans, chopped
- 2 carrots, peeled and finely chopped
- 1 onion, peeled and chopped
- 1 red pepper (bell pepper), de-seeded and chopped
- 1 small handful of fresh basil, chopped
- 1 tablespoon tomato purée (paste)
- 2 teaspoons paprika
- ½ teaspoon cayenne pepper
- 600mls (1 pint) hot vegetable stock (broth)

Method

Place all of the ingredients, except the spaghetti pieces and basil, into a slow cooker and stir well. Cook on high for around 4 hours or on low for 6-7 hours. Add in the spaghetti pieces and mix well. Cook for around 15 minutes or until the spaghetti has softened. Stir in the basil and serve into bowls. Enjoy.

Cream of Pumpkin Soup

Ingredients

900g (2lb) fresh pumpkin, peeled and de-seeded

2 teaspoons butter

1 onion, peeled and chopped

1/4 teaspoon nutmeg

1/4 teaspoon ground ginger

1/4 teaspoon cinnamon

600mls (1 pint) vegetable stock (broth)

150mls (5fl oz) double cream (or crème fraîche)

Sea salt

Freshly ground black pepper

SERVES 6

166 calories per serving

Method

Cut the pumpkin into chunks and place it in the slow cooker. Add in the butter, onion, nutmeg, ginger, cinnamon and stock (broth). Stir well. Cook on low for 5-6 hours or on high for 3-4 hours. Using a hand blender or food processor, blitz the soup until smooth. Stir in the cream and season with salt and pepper. Serve and enjoy.

Tomato & Quinoa Soup

Ingredients

400g (14oz) tinned tomatoes

400g (14oz) butterbeans

175g (6oz) quinoa, rinsed well

1 onion, peeled and chopped

1 bay leaf

1 small handful of fresh parsley, chopped

3 cloves garlic, crushed

1/2 teaspoon dried basil

1/2 teaspoon dried oregano

1/2 teaspoon dried thyme

750mls (1¼ pints) vegetable stock (broth)

Sea salt

Freshly ground black pepper

SERVES 4

171 calories per serving

Method

Place the tomatoes, quinoa, onion, butterbeans, garlic and herbs into a slow cooker. Pour in the vegetable stock (broth) and stir well. Season with salt and pepper. Cook on low for 7 hours or on high for 3 hours. Sprinkle in the parsley and remove the bay leaf before serving.

Thai Curry Soup

SERVES 4

418 calories per serving

Ingredients

450g (1lb) skinless chicken breasts, cut into strips

125g (4oz) frozen peas

2 tablespoons green curry paste

2 tablespoons fish sauce

1 tablespoon peanut butter

1 red pepper (bell pepper), deseeded and sliced

1 onion, finely chopped

2.5cm (1 inch) chunk of fresh ginger, peeled and finely chopped

1 small handful of coriander (cilantro)

400mls (14fl oz) coconut milk

600mls (1 pint) chicken stock (broth)

Juice of ½ lime

Method

In a bowl, combine the coconut milk with the curry paste, fish sauce, stock (broth) and peanut butter. Pour the mixture into a slow cooker. Add the chicken, onion, pepper and ginger. Cook on high for around 3 hours. Add the peas to the slow cooker and mix well. Cook for around 1 hour. Stir in the coriander (cilantro) and lime juice just before serving.

Cheesy Vegetable Soup

Ingredients

300g (11oz) crème fraîche
175g (6oz) Cheddar cheese, grated (shredded)
25g (1oz) cream cheese (full fat)
1 medium head of broccoli
2 carrots, peeled and grated (shredded)
1 onion, finely chopped
2 cloves of garlic, chopped
1 teaspoon dried mixed herbs
450mls (15 fl oz) chicken stock (broth)
Sea salt
Freshly ground black pepper

SERVES 4

312 calories per serving

Method

Place the carrots, onion, broccoli, cream cheese, stock (broth), garlic and herbs into a slow cooker and mix well. Cook on low for around 4 hours or on high for 2-3 hours. Stir in the crème fraîche. Transfer half of the soup to a deep bowl and using a hand blender, process it until it is smooth. Return the mixture to the slow cooker and stir it in thoroughly. Warm the soup further if you need to. Season with salt and pepper. Serve it into bowls with a sprinkling of cheese on top. Enjoy.

Pea Soup

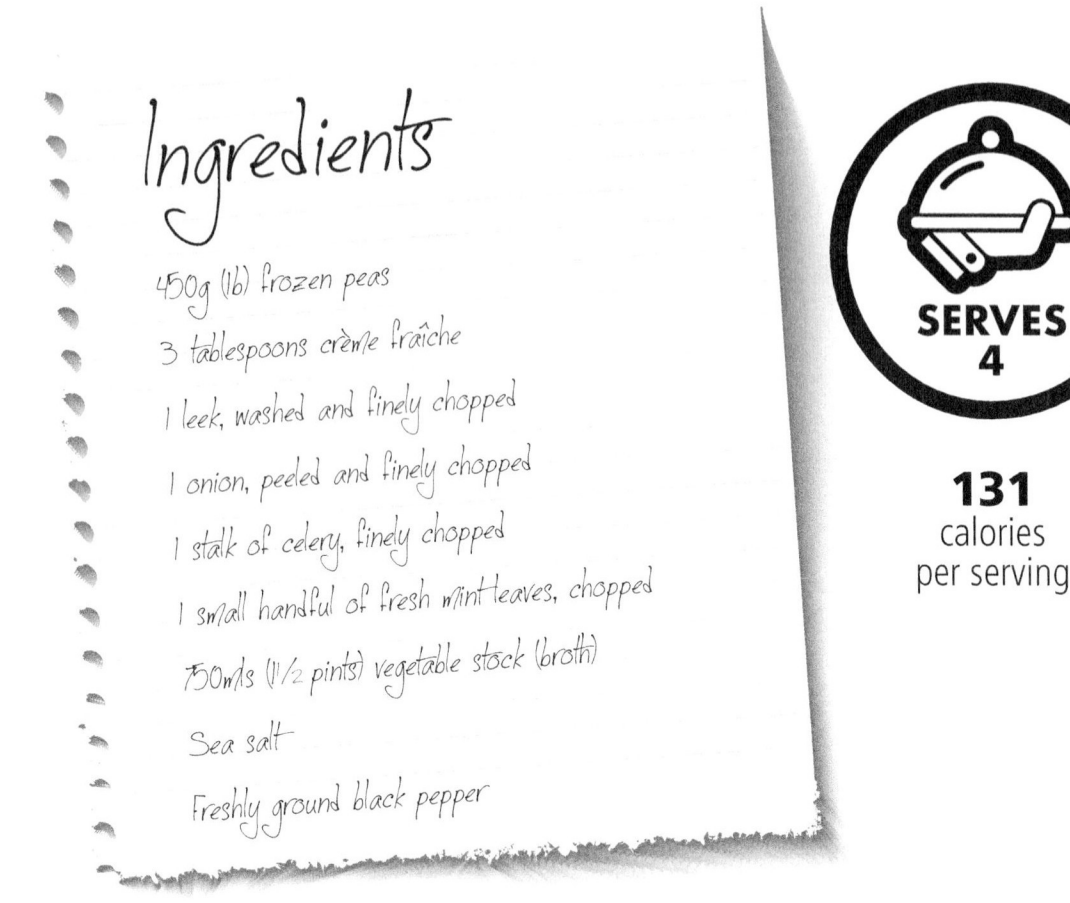

Ingredients

450g (1lb) frozen peas

3 tablespoons crème fraîche

1 leek, washed and finely chopped

1 onion, peeled and finely chopped

1 stalk of celery, finely chopped

1 small handful of fresh mint leaves, chopped

750mls (1½ pints) vegetable stock (broth)

Sea salt

Freshly ground black pepper

SERVES 4

131 calories per serving

Method

Place the onion, leek, celery and peas into a slow cooker and pour on the stock (broth). Cook on high for 3-4 hours or on low for 5-6 hours. Stir in the chopped mint and let it cook for 10 minutes. Season with salt and pepper. Using a hand blender, blitz the soup until smooth. Stir in the crème fraîche. Serve and eat straight away.

Creamy Celeriac Soup

Ingredients

2 onions, peeled and chopped

1 head of celeriac, peeled and finely chopped

1 potato, peeled and chopped

1 clove of garlic, chopped

1 teaspoon dried parsley

750mls (1¼ pints) hot vegetable stock (broth)

Sea salt

Freshly ground black pepper

2 tablespoons crème fraîche

SERVES 6

113 calories per serving

Method

Place all of the vegetables into a slow cooker and pour on the vegetable stock (broth). Cook on low for 6 hours or on high for around 3 hours. Using a hand blender, process the soup until smooth. Season with salt and pepper then stir in the crème fraîche. Serve and eat immediately.

MAIN MEALS

Chicken, Chorizo & Vegetable Casserole

Ingredients

450g (1lb) skinless chicken thighs

400g (14oz) tinned chopped tomatoes

225g (8oz) chickpeas (garbanzo beans), drained

100g (3½ oz) chorizo sausage, cut into bite-sized chunks

3 cloves garlic, chopped

2 red peppers (bell peppers), chopped

2 teaspoons ground coriander (cilantro)

½ teaspoon smoked paprika

1 onion, peeled and chopped

200mls (7fl oz) chicken stock (broth)

1 tablespoon olive oil

Sea salt

Freshly ground black pepper

A small handful of fresh coriander (cilantro), chopped

SERVES 4

428 calories per serving

Method

Heat the oil in a frying pan, add the chicken thighs and cook for around 5 minutes to brown them slightly on all sides. Add them to a slow cooker and all the remaining ingredients apart from the coriander (cilantro). Cook on a high heat for at least 5 hours or on low for 7 hours. Check that the chicken is cooked through. Sprinkle in the fresh coriander (cilantro) just before serving.

The Essential Slow Cooker Recipe Book

Slow Cooked Spiced Ham

Ingredients

- 400g (14oz) cannellini beans, drained
- 1 gammon joint, approx. 450g (1lb) in weight
- 1 large onion, peeled and chopped
- 3 stalks of celery
- 3 sprigs of thyme
- 2 carrots, peeled and sliced
- Zest of 1 orange
- 1 teaspoon dried parsley
- 1 teaspoon paprika
- 1/4 teaspoon chilli powder
- 1/2 teaspoon all-spice
- 450mls (16fl oz) vegetable stock (broth)
- Sea salt
- Freshly ground black pepper

SERVES 4

274 calories per serving

Method

Place the gammon in a slow cooker. Add all of the remaining ingredients and season with salt and pepper. Stir it well. Cook on a high setting for around 6 hours or until the ham is completely cooked and tender. Using 2 forks, pull apart the ham until it is nicely shredded. Serve with rice or new potatoes.

Beef Pot Roast

Ingredients

- 1 beef brisket joint, approximately 750g (approx. 1.6lb)
- 2 onions, peeled and roughly chopped
- 2 carrots, peeled and roughly chopped
- ½ small swede, cut into chunks
- 1 tablespoon tomato purée (paste)
- 1-2 teaspoons cornflour
- 1 bay leaf
- 250mls (9 fl oz) hot beef stock (broth)
- Sea salt
- Freshly ground black pepper

SERVES 4

477 calories per serving

Method

In a small bowl, mix together the hot beef stock (broth) and the tomato purée (paste). Place the beef into the slow cooker and add the vegetables and bay leaf. Pour the stock (broth) mixture over the top. Cook the meat on low for 5-6 hours or until it is tender. Pour the meat juices into a small saucepan. Mix the cornflour in a cup with a spoonful or 2 of cold water then stir it into the meat juices to thicken the gravy. If you prefer your gravy thicker add a little extra cornflour paste. Remove the bay leaf before serving. Serve with roast or mashed potatoes and a heap of fresh vegetables.

Chicken & Butternut Squash

Ingredients

175g (6oz) butternut squash, chopped
4 chicken breasts
2 cloves of garlic, crushed
2 x 400g (2 x 14oz) tinned chopped tomatoes
1 teaspoon ground cumin
1 teaspoon ground cinnamon
1 large onion, peeled and chopped
1 teaspoon ground ginger
½ teaspoon sea salt
¼ teaspoon ground black pepper
1 tablespoon olive oil

SERVES 4

262 calories per serving

Method

In a large bowl combine the ginger, cumin, cinnamon, salt and pepper. Coat the chicken in the mixture. Heat the oil in a saucepan and add the chicken and brown it on all sides for a few minutes. Place the chicken into a slow cooker and add in the garlic, tomatoes, onion and butternut squash. Cook on low for 7 hours or on high for 4 hours.

Thai Salmon Curry

Ingredients

- 4 skinless salmon fillets
- 2.5cm (1 inch) chunk of ginger
- 1 onion, peeled and chopped
- 1 stalk of lemongrass, outer leaves removed
- 1 small handful of coriander (cilantro) leaves
- 1 tablespoon Thai green curry paste
- 250mls (9 fl oz) coconut milk
- 200mls (7 fl oz) fish or vegetable stock (broth)
- Juice of 1 lime

SERVES 4

383 calories per serving

Method

Place the ginger, coriander (cilantro), lime juice, lemongrass, curry paste, coconut milk and onion into a food processor and blitz to a smooth paste. Place the salmon fillets into a slow cooker. Pour the curry mixture over the salmon. Cook on low for 2 ½ to 3 hours. The fish should be completely cooked and flake apart. Serve with rice and a sprinkling of coriander (cilantro).

Citrus Spiced Pork Fillet

Ingredients

- 1.35kg (3lb) pork fillet
- 5 cloves of garlic, finely chopped
- 3 teaspoons ground cumin
- 2 onions, peeled and sliced
- 2 teaspoons Cajun spice
- 1 teaspoon smoked paprika
- 1 teaspoon sea salt
- ½ teaspoon chilli powder (more if you like it spicy)
- Freshly squeezed juice of 3 large oranges
- 3 tablespoons red wine vinegar
- Zest and juice of 1 lemon

SERVES 6 approx.

434 calories per serving

Method

Place the garlic, chilli, cumin, Cajun spice, salt and paprika on a large plate and mix it together. Roll the pork fillet in the seasoning mixture and coat it completely. Transfer the pork to a slow cooker. Pour in the vinegar, orange juice, lemon juice and zest. Add the bay leaves and onion. Cook on low for 7 hours. Enjoy.

Chicken & Mushroom Casserole

SERVES 4

198 calories per serving

Ingredients

125g (4oz) medium sized mushrooms, halved
4 chicken breasts
3 cloves of garlic, chopped
2 stalks of celery, finely chopped
1 onion, peeled and chopped
1 tablespoon cornflour
2 teaspoons fresh parsley, chopped
600mls (1 pint) hot chicken stock (broth)
Sea salt
Pepper

Method

Place the cornflour in a cup and add just enough water to mix it to a smooth paste. Lay the chicken on the bottom of the slow cooker and scatter in the vegetables. Pour in the hot stock (broth) and mix well. Stir in the cornflour mixture, making sure it's dispersed throughout. Cook on low for 6-7 hours. Stir in the parsley and season with salt and pepper. Serve with brown rice or vegetables and potatoes.

Sweet & Sour Chicken

Ingredients

450g (1lb) chicken breasts, cut into chunks
400g (14oz) tin of pineapple in natural juice (not syrup)
8 spring onions, (scallions), chopped
2 tablespoons tomato purée (paste)
2 tablespoons cornflour
1 red pepper (bell pepper), deseeded and chopped
1 yellow pepper (bell pepper), deseeded and chopped
4 tablespoons white wine vinegar
2 tablespoons olive oil
2 teaspoons soy sauce

SERVES 4

346 calories per serving

Method

Drain the juice of the pineapple chunks and add the pineapple to a slow cooker and set aside the juice. Place the chicken, spring onions (scallions) and peppers into the slow cooker. In a small bowl, mix together the cornflour with 8 tablespoons of the natural pineapple juice you set aside together with the soy sauce, oil, vinegar and tomato purée (paste). Pour the mixture into the slow cooker. Cook on high for 5 hours. Serve with brown rice.

Prawn & Lemon Risotto

Ingredients

450g (1lb) prawns (shrimps), peeled and deveined
300g (11oz) risotto rice
200g (7oz) frozen peas, defrosted
25g (1oz) butter
1 medium onion, peeled and finely chopped
1/4 teaspoon chilli flakes
Zest and juice 1 lemon
750mls (1 1/4 pints) hot fish or vegetable stock (broth)
Sea salt
Freshly ground black pepper

SERVES 4

327 calories per serving

Method

Grease the inside of a slow cooker with butter. Place the rice, prawns (shrimps), onion, peas, chilli and lemon into the slow cooker and mix well. Pour in the hot stock (broth) and stir. Cook on low for 5-6 hours or until the rice is creamy and the prawns are pink throughout. Season with salt and pepper. Serve and enjoy.

Chestnut Mushroom & Red Pepper Risotto

Ingredients

450g (1lb) chestnut mushrooms, sliced

300g (11oz) risotto rice

50g (2oz) Parmesan cheese, grated

25g (1oz) butter

1 onion, chopped

1 red pepper (bell pepper), chopped

600mls (1 pint) hot vegetable stock (broth)

1 small handful of fresh basil leaves, chopped

SERVES 4

284 calories per serving

Method

Grease the inside of a slow cooker with butter. Place the rice, onion, mushrooms and red pepper (bell pepper) into the slow cooker and pour in the hot stock (broth). Cook on low for 4-5 hours or until the rice is creamy and soft. Stir in the parmesan cheese and basil leaves before serving.

Lemon Chicken

Ingredients

4 skinless chicken breasts
4 potatoes, peeled and chopped
3 carrots, peeled and chopped
3 cloves of garlic, crushed
1 onion, peeled and chopped
1 teaspoon of mixed herbs
25g (1oz) butter
600mls (1 pint) chicken stock (broth)
Juice of 1 lemon
Sea salt
Pepper

SERVES 4

389 calories per serving

Method

In a bowl, coat the chicken with the mixed herbs and season with salt and pepper. Heat the butter in a frying pan, add the chicken and quickly brown it slightly on either side. Place the chicken and all of the remaining ingredients into the slow cooker. Cook on high for 5-7 hours.

Chinese Beef & Broccoli

Ingredients

- 450g (1lb) beef steak, cut into strips
- 3 cloves of garlic, chopped
- 1 medium head of broccoli, broken into florets
- 2 tablespoons cornflour
- 1/4 teaspoon chilli flakes
- 350mls (12 fl oz) beef stock (broth)
- 100mls (3 1/2 fl oz) soy sauce
- 1 tablespoon sesame oil
- 1/2 teaspoon ground ginger
- 2 star anise
- Sea salt
- Freshly ground black pepper

SERVES 4

335 calories per serving

Method

Place the beef, soy sauce, stock (broth), chilli, garlic, oil, star anise and ginger into a slow cooker and stir well. Cook on low for around 4 hours. Mix the cornflour with 2-3 tablespoons of cold water and mix to a smooth paste. Stir the cornflour paste into the beef mixture. Cook for another 20 minutes or until the sauce has thickened. In the meantime, place the broccoli into a steamer and cook for 5 minutes. Add the broccoli to the mixture. Season with salt and pepper and serve.

Creamy Quinoa & Tomato Chicken

Ingredients

- 450g (1lb) chicken breast, diced
- 175g (7oz) quinoa
- 100g (3½ oz) cream cheese
- 6 medium tomatoes, chopped
- 2 red peppers (bell peppers), deseeded and chopped
- 1 onion, peeled and chopped
- 1 small handful of fresh basil leaves, chopped
- 600mls (1 pint) chicken or vegetable stock (broth)
- Sea salt
- Freshly ground black pepper

SERVES 4

337 calories per serving

Method

Place all of the ingredients, except the basil, salt and pepper into a slow cooker and mix well. Season with salt and pepper. Cook on low for 6-7 hours. Sprinkle the basil into the pot and give it a stir. Serve with a little basil on top.

Jambalaya

Ingredients

- 450g (1lb) chicken breast fillets, roughly chopped
- 450g (1lb) cooked peeled prawns (shrimps)
- 350g (12oz) smoked pork sausage, chopped
- 2 x 400g (2 x 14oz) tins chopped tomatoes
- 6 stalks of celery, finely chopped
- 2 teaspoons dried oregano
- 2 teaspoons dried parsley
- 2 teaspoons Cajun seasoning
- 1 onion, chopped
- 1 green pepper (bell pepper), chopped
- 1 teaspoon cayenne pepper
- 250mls (9 fl oz) chicken stock (broth)

SERVES 6

394 calories per serving

Method

Place all of the ingredients into a slow cooker and mix well. Cook on low for around 8 hours or on high for 5-6 hours. Serve with brown rice.

Lamb Shanks

Ingredients

- 50g (2oz) plain flour (all-purpose flour)
- 4 lamb shanks
- 4 fresh sprigs rosemary
- 3 large carrots, peeled and roughly chopped
- 2 onions, peeled and chopped
- 2 fresh bay leaves
- 1 tablespoon Worcestershire sauce
- 1 tablespoon tomato purée (paste)
- 1 clove of garlic, chopped
- 600mls (1 pint) beef or vegetable stock (broth)
- 2 tablespoons olive oil
- Sea salt
- Freshly ground black pepper

SERVES 4

359 calories per serving

Method

Place the flour into a bowl and coat the lamb shanks in it. Season with salt and pepper. Heat the oil in a frying pan and cook the lamb shanks on high for around 4 minutes to brown them. Place the lamb and the juices from the pan into a slow cooker. Add the remaining ingredients to the slow cooker. If necessary, add more hot water to make sure the lamb shanks are covered. Cook on low for 7-8 hours when the lamb is cooked and tender.

Tender 'Roast' Chicken

SERVES 4

396 calories per serving

Ingredients

1 large chicken

1 large onion, peeled and sliced

1 teaspoon paprika

Sea salt

Freshly ground black pepper

Method

Scatter the onion slices in the slow cooker and add the chicken. Sprinkle the chicken with the paprika and season it with salt and pepper. Cook on low for 6-8 hours on low. The chicken should be tender and falling off the bone. So simple and so delicious!

Pork, Apple & Ginger Chops

Ingredients

- 6 boneless pork chops
- 3 apples, peeled, cored and sliced
- 2 onions, peeled and finely chopped
- 1 teaspoon ground ginger
- 120mls (4fl oz) soy sauce
- 3 tablespoons tomato purée (paste)
- 2 cloves of garlic, chopped
- Sea salt
- Pepper

SERVES 6

213 calories per serving

Method

Place the chops on the bottom of a slow cooker. Place the soy sauce and tomato purée (paste) into a small bowl, mix it well then pour it over the pork. Scatter the onions, apples, ginger and garlic into the slow cooker. Cook on a low setting for around 6 hours. Season with salt and pepper. Serve and enjoy.

The Essential Slow Cooker Recipe Book

Tandoori Chicken

Ingredients

6 chicken breasts

1 tablespoon tandoori masala powder

3 tablespoons plain (unflavoured) yogurt

2 tablespoons lime juice

2 tablespoons olive oil

Sea salt

SERVES 6

278 calories per serving

Method

Place the tandoori powder, yogurt, lime and salt into a bowl and stir well. Add the chicken breasts and coat them thoroughly in the mixture. Cover them and allow them to marinade in the fridge for at least 2 hours. Coat a slow cooker in the olive oil. Transfer the chicken to the slow cooker and cook on low for 6 hours. Serve with rice and salad.

Paella

Ingredients

- 400g (14oz) tin of chopped tomatoes
- 450g (1lb) frozen seafood mix, defrosted
- 300g (11oz) risotto rice, rinsed
- 2 cloves of garlic, chopped
- 1 small handful of fresh parsley, chopped
- 1 onion, peeled and chopped
- 1 teaspoon paprika
- 1 teaspoon smoked paprika
- 1/2 teaspoon dried oregano
- 1/2 teaspoon dried thyme
- 2 tablespoon lemon juice
- 1 tablespoon olive oil
- 900mls (1½ pints) chicken or vegetable stock (broth)

SERVES 4

310 calories per serving

Method

Heat the olive oil in a frying pan, add the onion and garlic and cook for 4 minutes. Add in the rice, paprika, oregano and thyme and stir to coat the rice in the mixture. Transfer the ingredients to a slow cooker. Add in the stock (broth) and tomatoes. Cook on high for 2½ hours. Add in the defrosted seafood and cook for at least 40 minutes or until the fish is completely cooked through. Add in the parsley and lemon juice just before serving.

The Essential Slow Cooker Recipe Book

Chicken 'Fried' Rice

Ingredients

- 350g (12oz) basmati rice
- 100g (3½ oz) frozen peas
- 25g (1oz) butter
- 6 spring onions (scallions), chopped
- 4 chicken breasts, chopped
- 3 cloves of garlic, finely chopped
- 2 carrots, peeled and finely diced
- ½ teaspoon paprika
- ¼ teaspoon sea salt
- ¼ teaspoon pepper
- 2 tablespoons soy sauce
- 450mls (16fl oz) vegetable stock (broth)

SERVES 4

419 calories per serving

Method

Heat the butter in a frying pan, add the chicken and cook it for 5 minutes, stirring constantly. Transfer the chicken to a slow cooker. Add all the ingredients on top of the chicken. Cook on high for 3 hours or until the chicken is completely cooked and the rice is tender. If you need to, add a little extra stock if it requires longer cooking time. Check the seasoning before serving.

Chinese Pulled Pork

Ingredients

- 1kg (2lb 3oz) pork shoulder, cut into chunks
- 75g (3oz) brown sugar
- 5cm (2 inch) chunk of fresh ginger, peeled and chopped
- 2 cloves of garlic, chopped
- 2 red chillies, sliced
- 75mls (3 fl oz) red wine vinegar
- 75mls (3 fl oz) soy sauce
- 150mls (½ pint) sherry
- 150mls (½ pint) water
- 1 tablespoon olive oil

SERVES 6

526 calories per serving

Method

Heat the oil in a frying pan and add the red wine vinegar, sherry, soy sauce, sugar, garlic, ginger, chilli and water. Cook on a low heat for 5 minutes, stirring until it has dissolved. Place the pork into the slow cooker and add in sauce. Cook for around 4 hours on a high heat or 6 hours on a low heat. Serve with noodles, rice or stir fried vegetables.

Pork Vindaloo

Ingredients

750g (1lb 11oz) pork shoulder, cut into chunks

400g (14oz) tinned chopped tomatoes

6 small new potatoes, halved

2 onions, peeled and chopped

1 tablespoon tomato purée (paste)

1 cinnamon stick

3 cloves of garlic, chopped

3 cardamom pods

2 chillies

2cm (1 inch) chunk of fresh ginger roughly chopped

1 teaspoon cumin

1 teaspoon turmeric

1 teaspoon black pepper

100mls (3½ fl oz) chicken stock (broth)

3 tablespoons olive oil

2 tablespoons cider vinegar

SERVES 4

439 calories per serving

Method

Place the garlic, cardamom, chillies, ginger, cumin, turmeric, black pepper, olive oil and vinegar into a blender and process until smooth. Coat the pork in the mixture and allow it to marinate for at least 1 hour. Place the pork, potatoes, onions, tomato purée (paste), cinnamon, tomatoes and stock (broth) into the slow cooker and stir well. Cook on low for 4 hours or on high for 6-8 hours. Serve with rice or naan bread.

Bolognese

Ingredients

- 450g (1lb) minced (ground) beef
- 450g (1lb) passata
- 175g (6oz) small mushrooms, halved
- 3 cloves of garlic, chopped
- 2 courgettes (zucchinis), finely diced
- 1 onion, peeled and chopped
- 1 carrot, peeled and finely diced
- 1 teaspoon dried basil
- 1 teaspoon dried oregano
- 175mls (6fl oz) beef stock (broth)
- 2 teaspoons olive oil
- 1 small handful of fresh basil
- Sea salt
- Freshly ground black pepper

SERVES 4

332 calories per serving

Method

Heat the oil in a frying pan, add the onion and beef and brown it for 5 minutes. This step is optional as you can add the beef and onion directly to the slow cooker if you prefer. Transfer the beef and onion to a slow cooker and add all of the remaining ingredients, apart from the fresh basil. Cook on low for 8-9 hours. Stir in the fresh basil. Serve with whole-wheat or courgette (zucchini) spaghetti or roast vegetables. Enjoy.

The Essential Slow Cooker Recipe Book

Aromatic Pork Ribs

Ingredients

- 2 racks of pork ribs
- 2 onions, peeled and sliced
- 4 cloves of garlic, chopped
- 4 star anise
- 2 teaspoons ground ginger
- 150mls (5fl oz) hot water
- 2 tablespoons soy sauce
- Sea salt
- Pepper

SERVES 4

239 calories per serving

Method

Place the ribs into a slow cooker and add the garlic, onions, ginger, soy sauce and star anise. Season with salt and pepper. Pour in the hot water and cook on low for 6-8 hours. Serve the ribs with dips, pasta or salads.

Chicken Tagine

Ingredients

- 450g (1lb) chicken breasts, chopped
- 400g (14oz) chickpeas (garbanzo beans), drained
- 3 cloves of garlic, chopped
- 2 large carrots, peeled and chopped
- 1 large sweet potato (peeled and diced)
- 1 onion, peeled and chopped
- 2.5cm (1 inch) chunk of fresh ginger, peeled and chopped
- 1 teaspoon ground cinnamon
- 1 teaspoon ground turmeric
- 1 teaspoon ground coriander
- 1 teaspoon ground cumin
- 600mls (1 pint) chicken stock (broth)
- 2 teaspoons olive oil (optional)
- Sea salt
- Freshly ground black pepper

SERVES 4

435 calories per serving

Method

Heat the olive oil in a frying pan, add the chicken and onion and brown it for a few minutes. This step is optional as you can add the chicken and onion straight to the slow cooker – whichever you prefer. Place all of the ingredients into a slow cooker and stir well. Season with salt and pepper. Cook on a high setting for around 6 hours, or until the chicken is tender. Serve with rice, quinoa or couscous.

The Essential Slow Cooker Recipe Book

Beef & Barley Stew

Ingredients

500g (1lb 2oz) stewing steak, diced

100g (3½ oz) barley

1 onion, peeled and chopped

3 carrots, peeled and chopped

3 parsnips, peeled and chopped

900mls (1½ pints) hot beef stock (broth)

2 tablespoons Worcestershire sauce

1 tablespoon tomato purée (paste)

2 teaspoons olive oil (optional)

Sea salt

Freshly ground black pepper

SERVES 4

432 calories per serving

Method

Heat the oil in a frying pan, add the meat and onion and brown it for 5 minutes – this is optional, however as they can be added straight to the slow cooker if you'd prefer. Place the meat, barley and vegetables into the slow cooker. Pour in the stock (broth) and stir in the tomato purée and Worcestershire sauce. Season with salt and pepper. Cook on low for 8-9 hours or until the beef is really tender.

Chilli Chicken & Quinoa

Ingredients

- 2 x 400g (2 x 14oz) tins of chopped tomatoes
- 400g (14oz) kidney beans, drained
- 450g (1lb) chicken breasts, chopped
- 125g (4oz) quinoa
- 3 cloves of garlic, chopped
- 1 large red pepper (bell pepper), chopped
- 1 onion, peeled and chopped
- 1 teaspoon ground cumin
- 1 teaspoon chilli powder
- 1 teaspoon Cajun seasoning
- 600mls (1 pint) chicken stock (broth)
- Sea salt
- Freshly ground black pepper

SERVES 4

448 calories per serving

Method

Place all of the ingredients into a slow cooker and season with salt and pepper. Cook on low for 6-7 hours. Can be served with a dollop of guacamole, sour cream and a scattering of grated cheese.

Chicken Fajitas

Ingredients

- 400g (14oz) tinned chopped tomatoes
- 200g (7oz) Cheddar cheese, grated (shredded)
- 8 flour tortillas
- 5 cloves of garlic chopped
- 4 skinless chicken breasts, cut into strips
- 1 onion, peeled and chopped
- 1 red pepper (bell pepper), deseeded and chopped
- 1 green pepper (bell pepper), deseeded and chopped
- 1 yellow pepper (bell pepper), deseeded and chopped
- 2 teaspoons mild chilli powder
- 2 teaspoons ground cumin
- 2 teaspoons paprika
- 1 small handful of coriander (cilantro), chopped
- ½ teaspoon sea salt
- Juice of ½ lime

SERVES 4

466 calories per serving

Method

Add the chopped tomatoes to the slow cooker and stir in the onion, garlic, chilli powder, cumin, paprika and salt. Add the chicken breasts and coat them in the mixture. Scatter the chopped peppers over the top. Cook on high for around 4 hours, or until the chicken is tender and completely cooked. Stir in the coriander (cilantro) and lime juice. Serve into the tortillas with a sprinkling of cheese and you can add dollop of guacamole and sour cream too.

Lamb Hotpot

Ingredients

- 450g (1lb) potatoes, peeled and evenly sliced
- 450g (1lb) lean lamb steaks, cut into chunks
- 175g (6oz) mushrooms, sliced
- 1 onion, peeled and chopped
- ½ medium sized, swede, peeled and finely diced
- 3 carrots, peeled and finely diced
- 2 teaspoons cornflour
- 600mls (1 pint) beef stock (broth)
- 2 tablespoons Worcestershire sauce
- 2 teaspoons olive oil (optional)
- Sea salt
- Freshly ground black pepper

SERVES 4

401 calories per serving

Method

Heat the oil in a frying pan, add the meat and onion and brown it for 5 minutes. This step is optional as the lamb and onion can be added directly to the slow cooker. Transfer the lamb and onion to a slow cooker. Add the swede, carrots, mushrooms, Worcestershire sauce, stock (broth), salt and pepper. Mix together the cornflour with a tablespoon of water and stir it into the lamb mixture. Lay the potato slices in a circular pattern, with each slice just overlapping until the meat mixture is covered and all the potatoes have been used up. Cook on high for around 8 hours. You can add a knob of butter to the potatoes during cooking to keep them moist and golden if necessary.

The Essential Slow Cooker Recipe Book

Coconut & Coriander Chicken

Ingredients

- 4 chicken breasts, cut into chunks
- 1 teaspoon ground cumin
- 1 teaspoon ground coriander (cilantro)
- 1/2 teaspoon dried oregano
- 1/2 teaspoon chilli powder
- 4 cloves of garlic, finely chopped
- 200mls (7fl oz) coconut milk
- Sea salt
- Freshly ground black pepper

SERVES 4

238 calories per serving

Method

Place all of the ingredients into a slow cooker and stir them well. Cook on low for 6 hours, or until the chicken is cooked through. Serve with brown rice and vegetables.

Goulash

Ingredients

- 450g (1lb) stewing steak, cubed
- 400g (14oz) tinned chopped tomatoes
- 2 teaspoons tomato purée (paste)
- 2 cloves of garlic, chopped
- 2 red peppers, (bell peppers), deseeded and chopped
- 1 large onion, peeled and chopped
- 1 tablespoon paprika
- 1 large handful of fresh parsley
- 400mls (14fl oz) beef stock (broth)
- 150mls (5fl oz) crème fraîche
- 1 tablespoon olive oil

SERVES 4

332 calories per serving

Method

Heat the oil in a frying pan, add the steak, garlic and onions and brown them for a few minutes. Transfer it to a slow cooker. Add the remaining ingredients to the slow cooker, except the parsley and crème fraîche, and stir them well. Cook on low for around 6 hours. Sprinkle in the parsley and stir in the crème fraîche. Serve into bowls.

The Essential Slow Cooker Recipe Book

Cajun Pulled Pork

Ingredients

- 1.35kg (3lb) pork shoulder joint
- 300g (11oz) mushrooms, sliced
- 4 cloves of garlic, chopped
- 2 teaspoons Cajun seasoning
- 1 teaspoon chilli powder
- 1 teaspoon ground coriander (cilantro)
- 1 onion, peeled and chopped
- 1 handful of coriander (cilantro) leaves, chopped
- 900mls (1½ pints) chicken or vegetable stock (broth)

SERVES 8

371 calories per serving

Method

Place the Cajun seasoning and chilli powder on a large plate and coat the pork joint in the mixture. Transfer the pork joint to a slow cooker. Add the mushrooms, coriander (cilantro), garlic and onion and pour in the stock (broth). Cook on low for 7-8 hours or until the meat is tender and falling apart. Use 2 forks to pull the meat into shreds before serving.

Beef & Root Vegetables

Ingredients

- 1.35kg (3lb) beef silverside joint
- 400g (14oz) tinned chopped tomatoes
- 3 carrots, peeled and roughly chopped
- 2 parsnips, peeled and roughly chopped
- 3 teaspoons dried thyme
- 2 onions, sliced
- 1 small swede, peeled and roughly chopped
- 1 tablespoon cornflour
- 1 clove garlic, crushed
- 1 bay leaf
- 1 handful of fresh parsley, chopped
- 600mls (1 pint) beef stock (broth)
- 1 tablespoon olive oil
- Sea salt
- Freshly ground black pepper

SERVES 8

409 calories per serving

Method

Heat the oil in a large frying pan, add the meat and brown it well on each side. Remove the meat and place it in a slow cooker. Add the onions and garlic to the frying pan and cook them for 4 minutes then add them to the slow cooker. Surround the beef with the tinned tomatoes, vegetables and add in the herbs and stock (broth). Cook on low for 8 hours. Remove the beef from the slow cooker and set it aside, keeping it warm. Combine the cornflour with a tablespoon or two of cold water and mix it until smooth. Stir the cornflour mixture into the slow cooker and let it continue cooking for 10 minutes. Sprinkle in the parsley and mix well. Slice the beef and serve it along with the vegetables.

Chinese Chicken & Noodles

Ingredients

- 225g (8oz) egg noodles
- 4 chicken fillets
- 2.5cm (1inch) chunk of fresh ginger, peeled and chopped
- 2 cloves of garlic, chopped
- 1 onion, peeled and chopped
- 1 medium sized pak choi (bok choy), coarsely chopped
- 1 red pepper (bell pepper), deseeded and sliced
- 1 small handful of fresh coriander (cilantro) leaves
- 1 star anise
- ½ teaspoon chili powder
- 1 teaspoon fish sauce
- 1 tablespoon tomato purée (paste)
- 2 tablespoons soy sauce
- 350mls (12fl oz) hot chicken stock (broth)

SERVES 4

306 calories per serving

Method

Lay the chicken fillets on the bottom of a slow cooker. Add in the garlic, ginger, onion, chilli, star anise, fish sauce, purée (paste), soy sauce and stock (broth) and stir well. Cook on low for around 6 hours. Add the red pepper (bell pepper) and pak choi (bok choy). Cook for a further 20 minutes then sprinkle in the coriander (cilantro) and stir well. In the meantime, cook the noodles according to the instructions. Serve the noodles with the Chinese chicken on top.

Lamb Moussaka

Ingredients

450g (1lb) minced (ground) lamb

3 cloves of garlic, crushed

1 large onion, peeled and chopped

1 large aubergine (eggplant), cut into slices approx.1cm (1/2 inch) thick

1 teaspoon ground cinnamon

1 tablespoon tomato purée (paste)

1 tablespoon plain (all-purpose) flour

200mls (7fl oz) lamb or vegetable stock (broth)

1 tablespoon olive oil

FOR THE TOPPING:

225g (8oz) plain (unflavoured) yoghurt

75g (3oz) feta cheese, crumbled

3 eggs

pinch of grated nutmeg

SERVES 4

458 calories per serving

Method

Heat a tablespoon of oil in a frying pan, add the aubergine (eggplant) slices and brown them on each side. Remove them from the pan and set them aside. Add the lamb and onion to the frying pan and brown it for around 5 minutes. Transfer the lamb to a slow cooker. Add the stock (broth), garlic, spices, tomatoes, purée and flour. Cover the lamb mixture with slices of aubergine (eggplant) making sure it completely covers it. Cook on high for 6 hours or on low for 9 hours. In a bowl, mix together the eggs, yogurt, feta cheese and nutmeg. Spread the mixture on top of the aubergine. Continue cooking for around 1 hour until the mixture has set. Place the slow cooker bowl under a hot grill for 2 minutes to brown the topping. Serve with salad or a heap of vegetables.

Tender Five-Spice Beef

Ingredients

450g (1lb) braising steak, cut into strips

5cm (2 inch) chunk of fresh ginger, peeled and grated (shredded)

4 cloves of garlic, finely chopped

2 teaspoons Chinese five-spice powder

2 onions, peeled and thinly sliced

1 tablespoon cornflour

1 teaspoon chilli flakes

350mls (12fl oz) hot beef stock (broth)

4 tablespoon soy sauce

2 tablespoons olive oil

Sea salt

Freshly ground black pepper

SERVES 4

376 calories per serving

Method

Heat the oil in a frying pan, add the onions and cook for 4 minutes. Add the garlic, ginger and chilli and cook for 1 minute. Transfer the onion mixture to a slow cooker. Coat the beef in the five-spice powder then cook it in a hot pan for around 3 minutes to brown it. Place the meat in a slow cooker. Add in the stock (broth) and soy sauce. Cook for 4-5 hours on high. Mix the cornflour with 2 tablespoons of cold water and mix to a smooth paste. Stir the cornflour into the slow cooker. Let it continue cooking for 15 minutes. Serve with rice and vegetables.

Beef Bourguignon

Ingredients

- 450g (1lb) beef steak, cut into large chunks
- 350g (12oz) carrots, peeled and chopped
- 6 rashers streaky bacon, roughly chopped
- 3 cloves of garlic, peeled and chopped
- 2 sprigs of fresh thyme
- 1 onion, peeled and chopped
- 300mls (½ pint) red wine
- 300mls (½ pint) beef stock (broth)
- 2 tablespoons olive oil
- Sea salt
- Freshly ground black pepper

SERVES 4

438 calories per serving

Method

Heat a tablespoon of olive oil in a frying pan. Add the beef and cook for around 5 minutes to brown it, stirring occasionally. Season with salt and pepper. Add the bacon and onion and cook for 2 minutes. Remove them from the heat and add them to the slow cooker. Pour in the wine, stock (broth) together with the olive oil, garlic, carrots, and thyme. Cook on a low heat for 6-8 hours. Serve with pasta or potatoes.

Lamb & Mango Tikka

Ingredients

450g (1lb) lamb, diced

400g (14oz) tinned chopped tomatoes

100g (3½ oz) tikka curry paste

5cm (2 inch) chunk of fresh ginger, peeled and finely chopped

2 red onions, peeled and chopped

2 cloves of garlic, chopped

1 cinnamon stick

1 large mango, stoned, peeled and diced

300mls (½ pint) beef stock (broth)

1 tablespoon olive oil

A large handful of fresh coriander (cilantro), chopped

SERVES 4

458 calories per serving

Method

Heat the oil in a large frying pan. Add the lamb and cook for 5 minutes to brown it, stirring occasionally. Add the curry paste, garlic, ginger and cinnamon and cook for 2 minutes. Transfer the ingredients to the slow cooker. Add in the tomatoes, stock (broth) and cook on a low heat for 6-8 hours. Stir in the mango and cook for around 15 minutes or until it has warmed through. Add in the chopped coriander (cilantro) and remove the cinnamon stick. Serve with naan bread or rice.

Chicken Cacciatore

Ingredients

750g (1lb 11oz) mushrooms, halved
400g (14oz) tinned chopped tomatoes
4 skinless chicken breasts
3 tablespoons tomato purée (paste)
2 teaspoons dried oregano
3 cloves of garlic, chopped
1 onion, peeled and finely chopped
½ teaspoon cayenne pepper
200mls (7fl oz) hot chicken stock (broth)
2 tablespoons olive oil

SERVES 4

279 calories per serving

Method

In a bowl, mix together the hot stock (broth) and tomato purée. Place all the other ingredients into a slow cooker and pour the hot stock (broth) on top. Cook on low for around 6 hours. Serve with brown rice or quinoa and vegetables.

The Essential Slow Cooker Recipe Book

Pulled Chicken & Lettuce Wraps

Ingredients

- 4 skinless chicken breasts
- 4 large tomatoes, roughly chopped
- 4 medium sized onions, peeled and chopped
- 4 cloves of garlic, chopped
- 2 teaspoon ground ginger
- ½ teaspoon ground cinnamon
- 2 teaspoons fresh basil, chopped
- 1 teaspoon chilli powder
- 1 teaspoon cloves
- 1 iceberg or romaine lettuce, leaves separated
- 100mls (3½ fl oz) hot water

SERVES 4

244 calories per serving

Method

Place all of the ingredients, except the lettuce, into a slow cooker and stir well. Cook on low for around 6 hours. Use a fork to pull the chicken into shreds and mix it thoroughly with the other ingredients. To serve, spoon the pulled chicken mixture into lettuce leaves and fold them over. Alternatively, transfer it to a serving dish for everyone to help themselves.

Pork, Mustard & Apple Casserole

Ingredients

6 boneless pork chops

3 apples, peeled, cored and sliced

2 onions, peeled and sliced

1 small handful of fresh sage leaves, chopped

600mls (1 pint) hot chicken or vegetable stock (broth)

2 teaspoons wholegrain mustard

SERVES 6

199 calories per serving

Method

Lay the pork chops on the bottom of the slow cooker. Scatter the sage leaves over the top and add a layer of apples and onions. Add the mustard to the hot stock (broth) and mix well. Pour the stock (broth) into the slow cooker. Cook on low for 7 hours or until the chops are completely cooked. Serve with a heap of vegetables or mash.

The Essential Slow Cooker Recipe Book

Chicken Tikka Masala

Ingredients

- 1kg (2lb 3oz) chicken thighs, skin removed
- 400g (14oz) tinned chopped tomatoes
- 25g (1oz) flaked almonds
- 3 garlic cloves, crushed
- 2 tablespoons cornflour mixed with 2 tablespoons water
- 2 tablespoons freshly coriander (cilantro), chopped
- 2 teaspoons brown sugar
- 1 onion, peeled and chopped
- 1 tablespoon garam masala
- 2.5cm (1 inch) chunk of fresh ginger, peeled and chopped
- 1 tablespoon ground coriander (cilantro)
- 1 tablespoon ground cumin
- 150mls (5fl oz) natural yogurt
- 1 chilli pepper, chopped
- 100mls (3½ oz) single cream
- 2 tablespoons olive oil

SERVES 6

440 calories per serving

Method

In a bowl, mix together the cumin, ground coriander (cilantro) and yogurt in a bowl. Add the chicken and coat it in the mixture. Heat the oil in a frying pan. Add the chicken and cook for around 5 minutes to brown it. You will need to do this in batches. Remove it and set it aside. Add the onion, chilli, garlic, garam masala, ginger, sugar and tomatoes to the slow cooker and stir well. Add the chicken to the slow cooker. Cook on low for 6-8 hours. Add the mixed cornflour to the slow cooker and cook for 10 minutes, stirring occasionally until it has thickened. Add in the cream and stir well. Serve with a sprinkle of almonds and fresh coriander (cilantro). Serve with rice or nann bread.

Pork Curry

Ingredients

450g (1lb) pork steaks, cut into chunks

2 red peppers (bell peppers), deseeded and chopped

2 cloves of garlic, crushed

2 teaspoons ground ginger

1 stalk of lemongrass (inner leaves only)

1 large onion, peeled and chopped

1 red chilli pepper, deseeded and chopped

1 teaspoon ground cumin

1 teaspoon ground coriander

1 teaspoon paprika

½ teaspoon salt

½ teaspoon pepper

Juice of 1 lime

350mls (12fl oz) coconut milk

1 tablespoon olive oil

SERVES 4

415 calories per serving

Method

Heat the oil in a frying pan, add the pork and brown it for a few minutes. Transfer the pork to a slow cooker. Add all of the other ingredients, except the peppers, to the pot and stir really well. Cook for 6 hours or until the pork becomes tender. Add the peppers and cook for another 30 minutes. Remove the lemon grass before serving. Can be served with brown rice or cauliflower rice as a low carb alternative.

Chicken & Ham Pie

Ingredients

- 100g (3½ oz) thick cut ham, diced
- 100g (3½ oz) crème fraîche, optional
- 25g (1oz) butter
- 4 large chicken breasts, cut into chunks
- 2 leeks, chopped
- 2 tablespoons plain flour (all-purpose flour)
- 1 sheet of readymade puff pastry
- 1 onion, peeled and chopped
- 1 teaspoon dried thyme
- 1 teaspoon dried parsley
- 350mls (12fl oz) chicken stock (broth)
- 1 teaspoon olive oil

SERVES 4

552 calories per serving

Method

Heat the olive oil in a pan, add the chicken and onions and brown them for 5 minutes. Transfer the chicken to a slow cooker. Add the leeks and herbs to the mixture. Place the butter in the frying pan and allow it to melt. Remove it from the heat and whisk in the flour until it is smooth and creamy. Gradually add the stock (broth) to the butter mixture and whisk until smooth. Pour the stock (broth) into the slow cooker. Cook on low for 4-5 hours or until the chicken is tender. Allow the mixture to cool slightly. When ready to assemble the pie, stir the crème fraîche and ham into the chicken mixture. Transfer the chicken and ham filling to a pie dish. Roll out the pastry and cover the top of the dish, trimming around the edges. Preheat the oven to 180C/360F and cook the pie for 35-40 minutes or until the pastry is golden.

Slow Cooked Meat Loaf

Ingredients

675g (1½ lb) minced (ground) beef

100g (3½ oz) mushrooms, finely chopped

2 slices of brown bread, crumbed

2 eggs, beaten

1 teaspoon onion powder

1 teaspoon dried parsley

½ teaspoon salt

½ teaspoon dried sage

120mls (4fl oz) milk

1 teaspoon Worcestershire sauce

SERVES 6

247 calories per serving

Method

In a large bowl, combine the eggs, onion powder, breadcrumbs, salt, mushrooms, sage, parsley, milk and Worcestershire sauce. Add in the minced (ground) beef and mix it well. Using clean hands, shape the mixture into balls. Place it in the slow cooker and cook on low for 6 hours. Allow it to rest for 10 minutes before slicing and serving.

Salmon & Cannellini Mash

Ingredients

4 salmon fillets
2 x 400g (14oz) tins of cooked cannellini beans
2 tablespoons crème fraîche
1 onion, peeled and chopped
350mls (12fl oz) hot fish or vegetable stock (broth)
1 teaspoon mustard
Zest and juice of 1 lemon
1 small bunch of parsley
Sea salt
Freshly ground black pepper

SERVES 4

459 calories per serving

Method

Place the beans, onion, mustard, lemon and stock (broth) into a slow cooker and stir well. Season with salt and pepper. Lay the fish fillets on top of the beans. Cook on low for 2 hours or until the fish is completely cooked and is beginning to flake. Lift out the fish and set it aside. Drain off the liquid from the cooker, leaving the bean mixture in the cooker. Mash the cannellini beans together with the crème fraîche and stir in the parsley. Serve with the fish on top of the mash.

Chicken Stroganoff

Ingredients

300g (11oz) closed cup mushrooms, halved

300g (11oz) tinned condensed chicken soup

450g (1lb) skinless chicken breasts

1 teaspoon paprika

1 onion, peeled and chopped

150mls (1/4 pint) chicken stock (broth)

100mls (3½ fl oz) sour cream

2 tablespoons olive oil

A small bunch of fresh chives, chopped

SERVES 4

371 calories per serving

Method

Heat the oil in a large frying. Add the chicken breasts and onion and cook for 5 minutes or alternatively add them straight to the slow cooker if you don't wish to brown the chicken. Place all of the ingredients except the chives into a slow cooker and cook on low for around 6 hours. Scatter the chives into the stroganoff before serving with rice or pasta.

Chicken Wings

Ingredients

1.8kg (4lb) chicken wings, tips removed

FOR THE MARINADE:

2 tablespoons Worcestershire sauce
1 teaspoon paprika
1 teaspoon garlic powder
1 teaspoon sea salt
½ teaspoon Tabasco sauce
½ teaspoon chilli powder
175mls (6fl oz) soy sauce
Juice of 1 large lemon
Juice of 1 large orange

SERVES 6

492 calories per serving

Method

Place all of the ingredients for the marinade into a bowl and mix well. Add the chicken wings and coat them in the mixture. Allow them to marinade for at least half an hour and longer if you can. Transfer the chicken wings to a slow cooker. Cook on low for 5 hours. Serve into a platter for sharing. Enjoy.

Sausage Cassoulet

Ingredients

- 400g (14oz) tinned tomatoes
- 400g (14oz) butter beans, drained
- 400g (14oz) barlotti beans, drained
- 12 Cumberland sausages
- 8 rashers smoked streaky bacon
- 2 cloves of garlic, chopped
- 2 tablespoon tomato purée
- 2 teaspoons thyme leaves
- 1 onion, peeled and chopped
- 1 carrot, peeled and chopped
- 1 celery stalk, diced
- 1 teaspoon oregano, chopped
- 1 teaspoon smoked paprika
- 300mls (½ pint) vegetable stock (broth)
- 100mls (3½ fl oz) white wine
- 1 tablespoon olive oil

SERVES 6

484 calories per serving

Method

Heat a tablespoon of olive oil in the frying pan. Add the sausages and bacon and cook for about 5 minutes to brown them. Remove them from the heat and place them in the slow cooker. Pour the wine into the frying pan, stir it to remove the meat juices and add it to the slow cooker. Add in the remaining ingredients. Season with salt and pepper. Cook on a low heat for 6-8 hours. Serve with some crusty bread.

The Essential Slow Cooker Recipe Book

Spanish Chorizo & Peppers

Ingredients

500g (1lb 2oz) chorizo sausage, cut into slices

150g (5oz) tomato purée (paste)

6 cloves garlic, crushed

2 green peppers (bell peppers), seeded and chopped

2 red onions, peeled and chopped

600mls (1 pint) vegetable stock (broth)

1 teaspoon white wine vinegar

SERVES 6

433 calories per serving

Method

Scatter the sausage into a slow cooker; add the peppers, garlic, onion, tomato purée, vinegar, stock (broth) and water. Stir it well. Cook on low for 7 hours. This can be served on its own as a side dish or with vegetables, rice or potatoes.

Smoked Haddock & Pea Purée

Ingredients

275g (10oz) frozen peas

4 smoked haddock fillets

2 tablespoon crème fraîche or double cream (heavy cream)

1 tablespoon chopped fresh mint leaves

175mls (6fl oz) fish or vegetable stock (broth)

Sea salt

Freshly ground black pepper

SERVES 4

195 calories per serving

Method

Scatter the peas into a slow cooker and pour in the stock (broth). Set the haddock fillets on top of the peas. Cook on a high setting for 2 hours or until the fish is completely cooked, tender and flaky. Remove the fish from the slow cooker and set aside, keeping it warm. Add the mint, crème fraîche or cream. Using a hand blender or food processor blitz the peas until they are puréed. Season with salt and pepper. Serve the purée onto plates and place the haddock fillets on top. Eat straight away.

The Essential Slow Cooker Recipe Book

Turkey Meatballs & Tomato Sauce

Ingredients

FOR THE MEATBALLS:
- 450g (1lb) minced (ground) turkey
- 50g (2oz) whole wheat breadcrumbs
- 50g (2oz) Parmesan cheese, grated
- 1 egg
- 2 tablespoons fresh parsley, chopped
- 2 tablespoons fresh basil, chopped
- Sea salt
- Freshly ground black pepper

FOR THE TOMATO SAUCE:
- 2 x 400g (2 x 14oz) tinned chopped tomatoes
- 3 cloves of garlic, crushed
- 2 tablespoons chopped fresh parsley
- 1 tablespoon chopped fresh basil
- ½ teaspoon chilli flakes
- Freshly ground black pepper
- 1 teaspoon salt

SERVES 4

329 calories per serving

Method

In a large bowl, combine the turkey, breadcrumbs, Parmesan cheese, egg, parsley, basil, salt, and pepper. Shape the mixture into small balls. Pour all of the ingredients for the sauce into the slow cooker and mix well. Gently add the turkey balls to the tomato sauce and spoon some of the sauce over the top. Cook on low for 5 hours.

Satay Chicken

SERVES 4

326 calories per serving

Ingredients

- 450g (1lb) chicken breast fillet, cut into strips
- 75g (3oz) smooth peanut butter
- 6 cloves garlic, finely chopped
- 2 red peppers (bell peppers), deseeded and sliced
- 2.5cm (1 inch) chunk of fresh ginger, peeled and finely chopped
- 1 teaspoon chilli flakes (or less if you don't like it spicy)
- 250mls (9fl oz) chicken stock (broth)
- 75mls (3fl oz) soy sauce
- Juice of ½ lime

Method

Place all of the ingredients, except the lime, into a slow cooker and mix it well. Cook for about 6 hours on high and or until the chicken is completely cooked and tender. Stir in the lime juice. Serve with a green salad or brown rice.

Sausage Casserole

Ingredients

400g (14oz) tin of chopped tomatoes
100g (3½ oz) button mushrooms
8 good quality sausages
2 slices bacon
3 carrots, peeled and chopped
2 leeks, chopped
2 tablespoons cornflour
1 swede, peeled and chopped
1 tablespoon tomato purée (paste)
1 teaspoon paprika
1 teaspoon mixed herbs
300mls (½ pint) hot beef stock (broth)

SERVES 4

467 calories per serving

Method

Place the sausages under a hot grill (broiler) and brown them for around 4 minutes. Place the sausages, bacon, swede, mushrooms, carrots and leeks into a slow cooker. Add in the tomatoes, purée, paprika, herbs and stock (broth). Cook on low for 8 hours or on high for 4 hours. Mix the cornflour with 2 tablespoons of cold water and mix to a smooth paste. Stir the cornflour mixture into the casserole and allow it to cook for another 15 minutes.

VEGETARIAN RECIPES

Slow Cooked Mac and Cheese

Ingredients

350g (12oz) macaroni pasta

100g (3½ oz) mature cheddar, grated

50g (2oz) butter, cubed

50g (2oz) cream cheese

25g (1oz) Parmesan cheese

600mls (1 pint) whole milk

SERVES 4

654 calories per serving

Method

Place the pasta in a saucepan or colander and rinse it with boiling water. Shake it and let it drain. Put all of the ingredients into the slow cooker and stir well. Season with salt and pepper. Cook on a low heat for around 1 hour and stir it. Allow it to cook for around 30 minutes until the pasta is cooked and the cheese sauce has reduced a little. Remove the lid from the slow cooker and let it cook for another 10 minutes to help it reduce further or you can add a dash of milk if the sauce is too thick for your liking. Serve and enjoy with a little extra cheese if you like.

The Essential Slow Cooker Recipe Book

Vegetarian Lasagne

Ingredients

- 400g (14oz) tinned chopped tomatoes
- 125g (4oz) mozzarella cheese, chopped
- 6 lasagne sheets
- 2 tablespoons tomato purée (paste)
- 2 teaspoons vegetable bouillon (optional)
- 2 onions, peeled and sliced
- 2 cloves of garlic, chopped
- 2 large courgettes (zucchini), chopped
- 1 large aubergine, sliced lengthways
- 1 red pepper (bell pepper), deseeded and chopped
- 1 yellow pepper (bell pepper), deseeded and chopped
- A handful of fresh basil leaves, chopped
- 1 tablespoon olive oil

SERVES 4

328 calories per serving

Method

Heat the olive oil in a frying pan. Add the garlic, onions, courgettes (zucchinis), peppers, tomatoes, tomato purée, stock cubes and basil. Stir the mixture well and cook gently for 10 minutes. In the meantime, lay the aubergine slices in the bottom of the slow cooker and lay 3 lasagne sheets on top. Spoon around 1/3 of the tomato mixture on top. Add another layer of aubergine and lasagne sheets followed by another layer of the tomato mixture. Cook for around 3 hours or until the pasta is tender. Scatter the mozzarella cheese to the top and allow it to cook for around 5 minutes or until the cheese has melted. Serve and enjoy.

Slow Cooked Dahl

Ingredients

- 300g (11oz) yellow split peas
- 200g (7oz) fresh tomatoes, chopped
- 2.5cm (1 inch) chunk of fresh ginger, peeled and finely chopped
- 4 cloves of garlic, chopped
- 2 teaspoons ground cumin
- 2 teaspoons curry powder
- 1 teaspoon ground turmeric
- 1 onion, peeled and chopped
- 1 red chilli, finely sliced
- 1 small handful fresh coriander (cilantro) leaves, chopped
- 750mls (1½ pints) hot vegetable stock
- Sea salt and freshly ground black pepper

SERVES 4

140 calories per serving

Method

Place all of the ingredients except the coriander (cilantro) into a slow cooker and stir well. Cook on high for 4 hours. Season with salt and pepper. Stir in the coriander (cilantro). Serve the dahl on its own or with rice.

Sweet Potato, Peppers & Chickpeas

Ingredients

- 1 x 400g (14oz) tin of chickpeas (garbanzo beans)
- 1 x 400g (14oz) tin of chopped tomatoes
- 4 cloves of garlic, chopped
- 2 large courgettes (zucchinis), thickly chopped
- 2 sweet potatoes, peeled and chopped
- 2 teaspoons ground coriander (cilantro)
- 1 onion, peeled and chopped
- 1 medium aubergine (eggplant), thickly chopped
- 1 red pepper (bell pepper), deseeded and chopped
- 1 green pepper (bell pepper), deseeded and chopped
- 1 bunch of fresh basil, chopped
- Sea salt
- Freshly ground black pepper

SERVES 4

252 calories per serving

Method

Place all of the ingredients, except for the fresh basil, salt and pepper into a slow cooker and stir well. Cook on low for 6 hours. Season with salt and pepper. Sprinkle in the basil and mix well. Serve on its own or as a side dish.

Garlic, Tomato & Mushroom Spaghetti

Ingredients

400g (14oz) tin of chopped tomatoes

300g (11oz) spaghetti

225g (8oz) mushrooms, sliced

3 cloves of garlic, finely chopped

1 stalks of celery, finely chopped

1 bunch of fresh basil leaves, chopped

1 tablespoon olive oil

SERVES 4

164 calories per serving

Method

Place all of the ingredients, except the spaghetti and basil, into a slow cooker and stir well. Cook on low for 5-6 hours. When you are nearly ready to serve, cook the spaghetti according to the instructions. Transfer the spaghetti to the slow cooker and sprinkle in the fresh basil. Stir well before serving.

Cauliflower Korma

Ingredients

75g (3oz) green beans
75g (3oz) frozen peas
3 cloves of garlic, chopped
1 small cauliflower, broken into florets
1 onion, peeled and chopped
2 medium carrots, peeled and chopped
300mls (11fl oz) coconut milk
3 teaspoons mild curry powder
½ teaspoon sea salt
½ teaspoon cayenne pepper

SERVES 4

175 calories per serving

Method

In a bowl, mix the coconut milk with the curry powder and stir to combine them. Place this and the ingredients into a slow cooker and stir well. Cook on low for 5-6 hours. Serve with brown rice.

Caribbean Citrus Squash

Ingredients

- 3 onions, finely sliced
- 3 cloves of garlic, peeled and chopped
- 2 butternut squash, peeled and chopped
- 2 teaspoons ground ginger
- 1 red chilli, finely chopped
- 1 small handful of fresh coriander (cilantro), chopped
- 200mls (7 fl oz) vegetable stock (broth)
- 2 tablespoons sesame oil
- Juice of 2 large orange
- Juice of 2 limes
- Sea salt
- Freshly ground black pepper

SERVES 4

200 calories per serving

Method

Place all of the ingredients, except the coriander (cilantro), salt and pepper into a slow cooker and stir them well. Cook on low for 4 hours. Season with salt and pepper. Stir in the fresh coriander (cilantro) just before serving.

Slow Cooked 'Baked' Potatoes

SERVES 6

231 calories each

Ingredients

6 large baking potatoes

2 teaspoons butter

Sea salt

Method

Rub a little butter into the skin of each potato then sprinkle it with salt. Wrap each of the potatoes in tin foil, making sure they are completely sealed. Cook on high for around 4 hours or on low for 8 hours. Remove the potatoes from the slow cooker and remove the foil – take care as the potatoes will be piping hot. Serve with toppings such as cheese and chilli or avocado and bacon.

Stuffed Peppers

Ingredients

400g (14oz) tinned cannellini beans, drained

100g (3½ oz) brown rice

3 cloves of garlic, chopped

2 red peppers (bell peppers), top removed and de-seeded

2 yellow peppers (bell peppers), top removed and de-seeded

1 onion, peeled and finely chopped

1 teaspoon paprika

A handful of fresh basil

600mls (1 pint) vegetable stock (broth)

Sea salt

Freshly ground black pepper

SERVES 4

202 calories per serving

Method

Place the beans, rice, garlic, onion, basil and paprika into a bowl and mix well. Season with salt and pepper. Scoop some of the mixture into each of the peppers and place the lid back onto the peppers. Pour the hot vegetable stock (broth) into a slow cooker. Gently lower the peppers into the stock, keeping them upright. If your slow cooker is large you can roll up some tin foil into balls and insert them alongside the peppers to keep them upright. Cook on low for around 5 hours or until the rice is soft. Serve and enjoy.

Butternut Squash & Bean Casserole

Ingredients

400g (14oz) tinned cannellini beans, drained

400g (14oz) tinned chickpeas, drained

400g (14oz) tinned chopped tomatoes

350g (12oz) butternut squash, peeled and chopped

250g (9oz) mini peppers, deseeded and halved

75g (3oz) toasted pine nuts

1 onion, peeled and chopped

A handful of fresh basil leaves, chopped

2 tablespoons olive oil

SERVES 4

413 calories per serving

Method

Place the cannellini beans, chickpeas, tomatoes, squash, onion, peppers and olive oil into a slow cooker and stir well. Cook on a low heat for around 4 hours. Stir in the basil and serve with a sprinkling of pine nuts on top.

Vegetable & Cannellini Bean Rice

Ingredients

- 400g (14oz) tin of cannellini beans, drained
- 200g (7oz) basmati rice, rinsed
- 175g (6oz) butternut squash, peeled and chopped
- 6 spring onions (scallions), chopped
- 2 medium tomatoes, finely chopped
- 1 green pepper (bell pepper), deseeded and chopped
- 1 red chilli, deseeded and finely chopped
- 1 small handful of chopped basil
- ½ teaspoon ground allspice
- ½ teaspoon garlic powder
- ½ teaspoon salt
- ½ teaspoon pepper
- 750mls (1¼ pints) vegetable stock (broth)

SERVES 4

243 calories per serving

Method

Place the rice and vegetables into a slow cooker. Add in the allspice, garlic, chilli, salt and pepper and the stock (broth) and mix well. Cook on high for 1 ¾-2 hours. Sprinkle in the basil and stir. Serve into bowls and enjoy.

Ratatouille

Ingredients

- 225g (8oz) cherry tomatoes
- 3 medium sized courgettes (zucchinis)
- 3 cloves of garlic, chopped
- 1 onion, peeled and chopped
- 1 aubergine (eggplant), chopped
- 2 red peppers (bell peppers), de-seeded and chopped
- 1 teaspoon dried Herbs de Provence
- 175mls (6fl oz) vegetable stock (broth)
- A handful of fresh basil, chopped
- 1-2 teaspoons cornflour
- 2 teaspoons olive oil

SERVES 4

111 calories per serving

Method

Heat the olive oil in a frying pan, add the chopped onion and cook for 5 minutes. Transfer the onions to a slow cooker. Add all the remaining ingredients to the slow cooker, apart from the cornflour and the basil. Cook on a high setting for 3 hours. Mix the cornflour with a tablespoon of cold water and stir it into the ratatouille. Cook for another 30 minutes. Stir in the fresh basil before serving.

Baked Beans

Ingredients

2 x 400g (2 x 14oz) tins of cannellini beans, drained

2 x 400g (2 x 14oz) tins of chopped tomatoes

25g (1oz) butter

4 strips of pancetta, finely chopped

1 large onion, finely chopped

250mls (9 fl oz) vegetable stock (broth)

SERVES 4

306 calories per serving

Method

Heat the butter in a frying pan, add the onion and pancetta and cook for a few minutes until the onion has softened. Transfer them to a slow cooker. Add the tomatoes, beans and vegetable stock (broth). Cook on low for 7 hours. Serve on their own or as a side dish. Makes a great sugar-free alternative to tinned baked beans.

Braised Savoy Cabbage & Peas

Ingredients

275g (10oz) frozen peas

1 head of savoy cabbage, finely chopped

1 large onion, peeled and chopped

200mls (7fl oz) vegetable stock (broth)

Sea salt

Freshly ground black pepper

SERVES 4

89 calories per serving

Method

Place all of the ingredients into a slow cooker and stir well. Cook on high for 1-½ -2 hours. Season with salt and pepper, if required. Serve as a perfect accompaniment to meat, chicken and fish dishes.

Slow Cooked Autumn Vegetables

Ingredients

- 150g (5oz) cherry tomatoes, halved
- 150g (5oz) button mushrooms
- 125g (4oz) soya beans
- 125g (4oz) peas
- 3 cloves of garlic, peeled and chopped
- 2 carrots, peeled and roughly
- 1 whole beetroot, washed and roughly chopped
- 1 butternut squash, peeled and cut into chunks
- 1 medium broccoli, broken into florets
- 1 teaspoon dried thyme
- 1 teaspoon dried oregano
- 1 tablespoon olive oil
- Sea salt
- Freshly ground black pepper

SERVES 4

192 calories per serving

Method

Place all of the ingredients, except the tomatoes, into a slow cooker and mix them well. Cook on low for 3 hours. Add the tomatoes to the slow cooker and continue cooking for 30 minutes. Serve on its own or as an accompaniment to meat, chicken and fish dishes.

Red Cabbage

Ingredients

2 apples, peeled cored and chopped

1 onion, peeled and chopped

1 head of red cabbage, finely chopped

½ teaspoon allspice

½ teaspoon cinnamon

120mls (4fl oz) red wine vinegar

Pinch of salt

SERVES 6

51 calories per serving

Method

Place all of the ingredients into the bowl of a slow cooker and give them a stir. Cook on low for 6-7 hours. Can be served warm or you can let it cool then spoon it into a lidded jar and store, ready to serve cold.

Sugar-Free Pasta Sauce

Ingredients

2 x 400g (2 x 14oz) tinned chopped tomatoes

6 medium tomatoes, preferably on the vine, chopped

2 medium courgettes (zucchinis), chopped

1 small carrot, peeled and chopped

1 onion, peeled and chopped

1 bay leaf

1 handful fresh parsley, chopped

4 cloves of garlic, chopped

1/2 teaspoon pepper

1/2 teaspoon salt

2 teaspoons dried mixed herbs

SERVES 8

46 calories per serving

Method

Place all of the ingredients into a slow cooker and cook on high for 3 hours. Remove the bay leaf and discard it. Use a hand blender or food processor and blitz the sauce until smooth. It can be added to pasta and meat dishes or easily stored in the fridge or freezer until ready to use. You can also double the quantities to make a larger batch if you want to freeze and store some.

Cranberry & Orange Sauce

Ingredients

400g (14oz) bag of fresh cranberries

1 cinnamon stick

Freshly squeezed juice of 3 large oranges

1-2 teaspoons stevia powder or liquid

SERVES 8

189 calories per batch

Method

Place all of the ingredients into a slow cooker and cook on low for 5 hours then remove the lid and continue cooking for another hour. Remove the cinnamon stick. Store in an airtight jar until ready to use. The perfect accompaniment to roast turkey!

DESSERT & PUDDING RECIPES

Chocolate Brownies

Ingredients

- 125g (4oz) self-raising flour
- 75g (3oz) hazelnuts, chopped
- 50g (2oz) 100% cocoa powder
- 25g (1oz) butter
- 4 egg whites
- 2 tablespoons cacao nibs (or unsweetened chocolate chips)
- 2 large apples, peeled, cored and chopped
- 2 medium, ripe bananas, mashed to a pulp
- 1 teaspoon stevia sweetener (optional)
- 1 teaspoon baking powder
- Extra butter for greasing

MAKES 24

90 calories each

Method

First, you need to line the slow cooker with greaseproof paper. Cut out an oval shaped piece of greaseproof paper by drawing around the bottom of the bowl. Insert the paper and coat it and the sides of the cooker with butter. Place the chopped apples into a saucepan with just enough hot water to cover the bottom of the pan and gently warm them for 10 minutes until the apple has softened then mash it until smooth then set it aside. Place the cocoa powder, baking powder, hazelnuts, flour, cacao nibs (chocolate chips) and stir. In another bowl, mix together the butter, bananas, eggs, apples, stevia (if using) and mix well. Mix the wet ingredients into the dry and combine them thoroughly. Transfer the mixture to the slow cooker. Cook on low for 4 hours. Use a palette knife cut the mixture from the sides of the slow cooker them tip it out. Allow it to cool before slicing and serving.

Lemon & Coconut Rice Pudding

Ingredients

100g (3½ oz) short grain brown rice

2 tablespoons toasted coconut chips (unsweetened)

1-2 teaspoons stevia sweetener

1 teaspoon vanilla extract

1 teaspoon grated (shredded) lemon zest

½ teaspoon salt

600mls (1 pint) coconut water

400mls (14fl oz) coconut milk

Butter for greasing

SERVES 4

299 calories per serving

Method

Coat the inside of a slow cooker with butter. Add the rice, coconut water, coconut milk, stevia, vanilla and salt and mix the ingredients well. Cook on low for 4-5 hours. Sprinkle in the lemon zest and stir. Allow the lemon to infuse for a few minutes. Serve into bowls and garnish with toasted coconut chips. You can all serve with fresh fruit, hot or cold.

Chocolate Rice Pudding

Ingredients

100g (3½ oz) short grain brown rice

2-3 teaspoons stevia sweetener

1½ tablespoons 100% cocoa powder

½ teaspoon ground cinnamon

½ teaspoon ground nutmeg

1 teaspoon vanilla extract

750mls (1¼ pints) milk

150mls (5fl oz) double cream (heavy cream)

SERVES 4

395 calories per serving

Method

Place the rice, milk, cocoa powder, cream and stevia into a slow cooker and stir well. Sprinkle in the cinnamon, nutmeg and vanilla extract and mix together. Cook on low for 4-5 hours or until the rice is soft and creamy. Serve on its own or add some fruit such as chopped fresh apricots or a handful of berries.

Banana Bread

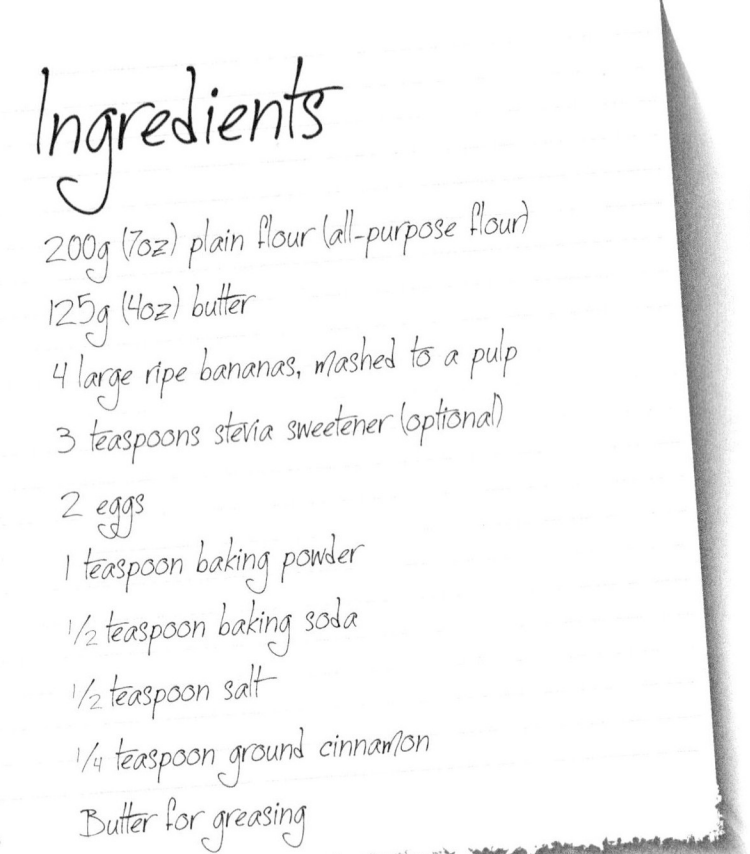

Ingredients

200g (7oz) plain flour (all-purpose flour)
125g (4oz) butter
4 large ripe bananas, mashed to a pulp
3 teaspoons stevia sweetener (optional)
2 eggs
1 teaspoon baking powder
½ teaspoon baking soda
½ teaspoon salt
¼ teaspoon ground cinnamon
Butter for greasing

SERVES 6

271 calories per serving

Method

In a bowl, combine the eggs, butter and stevia (if using). Stir in the bananas, flour, cinnamon, baking soda, baking powder and salt and mix really well. Grease a loaf tin which sits easily inside your slow cooker. Spoon the bread mixture into the tin. Cook on low for 4 hours. Allow it to cool then slice and serve.

Stuffed Apples

Ingredients

4 large apples, core removed

2 teaspoons stevia sweetener

100g (3½ oz) walnuts, finely chopped

50g (2oz) oats

25g (1oz) butter, cut into flakes

½ teaspoon ground cinnamon

SERVES 4

345 calories per serving

Method

In a bowl, combine the oats, butter, stevia, cinnamon and walnuts. Mix until well combined. Spoon some of the mixture into the hole where the core was removed from the apples. Place the apples upright in a slow cooker and add just enough water to cover the bottom of the slow cooker. Cook on low for 3 hours. Serve with yogurt, cream or crème fraîche. Enjoy.

Poached Peaches

Ingredients

100g (3½ oz) fresh blueberries

4 large peaches (or 6 small), halved and stone removed

1 teaspoon ground ginger

90mls (3fl oz) freshly squeezed orange juice

SERVES 4

68 calories per serving

Method

Lay the peach halves, flat side down, on the bottom of a slow cooker. Sprinkle on the ginger, pour in the orange juice and add the blueberries. Cook on low for 90 minutes. Serve on their own or with a dollop of plain yogurt or crème fraîche.

Fruit Compote

Ingredients

900g (2lb) frozen mixed berries

1½ tablespoons cornflour

90mls (3 fl oz) freshly squeezed orange juice

1-2 teaspoons stevia sweetener (optional)

2 tablespoons water

SERVES 6

54 calories per serving

Method

Place the berries, orange juice and stevia into a slow cooker and stir well Cook on high for 90 minutes. Mix together the cornflour and water and stir until it becomes smooth. Pour the mixture into the berries. Allow it to cook for 15 minutes, stirring occasionally. Serve with a dollop of Greek yogurt or crème fraîche.

Fresh Custard & Raspberries

Ingredients

200g (7oz) raspberries

4 large eggs, preferably free-range

2-3 teaspoons of stevia sweetener, or to taste

1 teaspoon cornflour

1 teaspoon vanilla extract

450mls (16fl oz) full-fat milk

Hot water

SERVES 4

68 calories per serving

Method

Mix the cornflour with a tablespoon of the milk until it becomes smooth. Gently whisk the eggs and stir in the cornflour mixture, milk, stevia and vanilla extract. Use a heatproof dish which fits inside your slow cooker and pour the egg mixture into it. Cover the dish with silver foil and place it in the centre of the slow cooker. Pour hot water into the slow cooker until it comes around half way up the dish inside it. Cook on high for around 3 hours. Remove the custard from the cooker and pour it into bowls. Allow it to cool slightly then sprinkle on the raspberries. Serve and eat immediately.

You may also be interested in other titles by
Erin Rose Publishing
which are available in both paperback and ebook.

Quick Start Guides

Healthy Gut Diet Recipe Book
A Quick Start Guide To Improving Your Digestion, Health And Wellbeing
PLUS over 80 Delicious Gut-Friendly Recipes

The Essential Low FODMAP Diet Cookbook
A Quick Start Guide To Relieving the Symptoms of IBS Through Diet
Improve Your Digestion, Health And Wellbeing
PLUS over 75 IBS-Friendly Recipes

The Essential Diabetes Diet Cookbook
A Quick Start Guide To Managing Your Diabetes Through Diet

The Alkaline Diet Solution
A Quick Start Guide To The Alkaline Diet
Lose Weight, Improve Your Health and Feel Great!
PLUS over 90 Alkaline Friendly Recipes

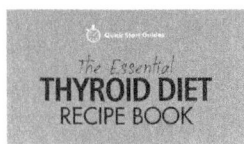

The Essential Thyroid Diet Recipe Book
A Quick Start Guide To Healing Your Thyroid Through Diet. Lose Weight And Feel Great With Delicious Thyroid Friendly Recipes

The Essential Sirt Food Diet Recipe Book
A Quick Start Guide to Cooking on the SIRT Food Diet
Over 100 Easy and Delicious Recipes to Burn Fat, Lose Weight, Get Lean and Feel Great!

What Can I Eat? On A Dairy Free Diet
A Quick Start Guide To Quitting Dairy and Lactose. Lose Weight, Feel Great and Increase Your Energy!
PLUS 100 Delicious Dairy-Free Recipes

Lower Cholesterol Diet
A Quick Start Guide To Lower Cholesterol
Improve Your Health and Feel Great
PLUS over 100 Delicious Cholesterol Lowering Recipes

The Vegan 15 Minute Cookbook
Over 100 Simple And Delicious Vegan Recipes For Everyone

The Essential Roasting Tin Cookbook
Over 80 Easy And Delicious One Dish, No-Fuss Oven Recipes

Blood Sugar Diet Diary
Daily Diary To Track Foods, Weight Loss and Wellbeing On The Blood Sugar Diet

Diabetes Diet Diary

My Diet Diary
Daily Diet, Health And Fitness Diary To Track Weight Loss And Well-being

Low FODMAP Food Diary

Sugar-Free Diet Diary
Daily Diary For Quitting Sugar, Losing Weight and Feeling Great

Food Diary
Daily Diary To Track Diet And Symptoms To Beat Food Intolerances And Digestive Disorders

Printed in Great Britain
by Amazon